A Reference Publication in Literature

Ronald Gottesman, *Editor*

Saul Bellow:
A Reference Guide

Robert G. Noreen

G. K. HALL & CO., 70 LINCOLN STREET, BOSTON, MASS.

Library of Congress Cataloging in Publication Data

Noreen, Robert G
    Saul Bellow : a reference guide.

    (Reference publications in literature)
    Includes index.
    1. Bellow, Saul--Bibliography. I. Series.
Z8087.8.N66   [PS3503.E4488]   016.813'5'2   77-22551
ISBN 0-8161-7990-5

This publication is printed on permanent/durable acid-free paper
MANUFACTURED IN THE UNITED STATES OF AMERICA

Contents

Introduction

For some years Saul Bellow has been considered by literary critics and the well-read public alike to be America's most important living novelist, the heir and successor to Faulkner and Hemingway. The award of the 1976 Nobel Prize for Literature, has assured his international reputation as well. Since the publication of his first novel, Dangling Man, in 1944, he has been recognized as a significant voice in modern fiction, and the growing body of criticism devoted to his work has reached massive proportions. Eight full-length books, four collections of essays, twenty-five doctoral dissertations, and hundreds of critical essays and reviews now have the works of Bellow as their subject. The purpose of this reference guide is to organize this body of criticism in the hope that it may serve three functions: to chronicle the diversity of reactions to one of America's finest novelists, to assist students and general readers with a guide to the most useful explications of Bellow's work, and to facilitate the research of scholars and critics who in the future study Bellow and his works.

Saul Bellow, the youngest of four children, was born in Lachine, Quebec, a suburb of Montreal, in 1915, of Russian Jewish immigrant parents. His family moved to Chicago in 1924 where Bellow attended high school and the University of Chicago; he received his bachelor's degree with honors in anthropology and sociology at Northwestern University in 1937. For most of his professional life Bellow has been associated with colleges and universities; he has taught at Bard College, New York University, the University of Minnesota, and Princeton. In 1963 he began teaching at the University of Chicago, receiving an appointment to the prestigious Committee on Social Thought of which he was chairman from 1970 to 1976. In 1976 he was designated the Raymond W. and Martha Hilpert Grunner distinguished service professor at the University of Chicago.

Bellow has been the recipient of many honors and awards, including a Guggenheim Fellowship (1948), the National Institute of Arts and Letters Award (1952), the National Book Award for Fiction (1954, 1965, 1970), the Friends of Literary Fiction Award (1960), the International Literary Prize (1965), the B'nai B'rith Jewish Heritage Award (1968), the Croix de Chevalier des Arts et Lettres (the highest literary distinction awarded by France to non-citizens, 1968), the Pulitzer Prize

for Fiction (1976), and the Nobel Prize for Literature (1976). He
was elected by the National Council on the Humanities to be the 1977
Jefferson Lecturer in the Humanities.

Bellow has published eight novels, five plays, and a number of
short stories and essays since the early 1940's. His first short
story, "Two Morning Monologues," was published in 1941, his first
novel, Dangling Man, appeared in 1944. His second novel, The Victim,
appeared in 1948, and the third, The Adventures of Augie March, in
1953, for which he won the National Book Award. Seize the Day followed in 1956, and Henderson the Rain King in 1959. Herzog, published in 1963, won the National Book Award and the International
Literary Prize. A collection of short stories, Mosby's Memoirs and
Other Stories, appeared in 1968. Mr. Sammler's Planet, 1969, was the
third winner of the National Book Award, and Humboldt's Gift, 1975,
won the Pulitzer Prize for Literature. To Jerusalem and Back: A
Personal Account, published in 1976, is based on a journal Bellow
kept on a 1975 visit to Israel.

Bellow's play, "The Last Analysis," had a short run on Broadway in
1964 as did his three short plays, "Under the Weather," in 1966.
Bellow has contributed fiction to Partisan Review, Harper's Bazaar,
the New Yorker, Esquire, Atlantic, and several literary quarterlies.
He has published criticism in Encounter, New Republic, New Leader,
New York Times Book Review, Horizon, Harper's, Commentary, Partisan
Review, Reporter, Nation, and other periodicals. In the early six-
ties he briefly edited the periodical, The Noble Savage.

Bellow's contributions to contemporary American literature have
thus been considerable, and the characters he has created have become
firmly established in the American imagination. His novels portray
characters who, confused and lost, are in the midst of serious crises
of identity and faith, striving to make sense of life and death and
the mystery of man's existence. In "Distractions of a Fiction Writer"
Bellow wrote,

> Why were we born? What are we doing here? Where
> are we going? In its eternal naivete the imagina-
> tion keeps coming back to these things. It does
> this when we have an agreed picture (of the mean-
> ing of the universe) and when we do not. For it
> isn't an agreed picture that makes man interesting
> to himself. It isn't history and it isn't culture:
> the interest is intrinsic.

In all of his writing Bellow has returned again and again to these
probing questions. In considering these same questions many novelists and poets since World War II have been led to a philosophy of
nihilism with its cynical view of man and his possibilities. But
Bellow, unlike so many of his contemporaries, has not allowed these
questions to cause either overwhelming despair in himself or his

works. He has represented the wretchedness and absurdity of man's condition and his many failures, but he has not been content to dwell upon this wretchedness alone. For no matter how absurd one of his protagonists may appear, Bellow still portrays him as being "interesting to himself." This interest has led his striving heroes not toward a goal of success, nor even enlightenment, but rather toward an acceptance of the dignity of life.

One of Bellow's major achievements has thus been the creation of resilient heroes, those who maintain faith in themselves and the dignity of life in spite of the absurdity of their condition. For some of his protagonists this is no small task, for they, indeed, have very little to be optimistic about; they have none of the qualities of the successful, self-confident, super-American male: they are failures and washouts—poor husbands, indifferent lovers, weak parents, ungrateful children. They seem subject to even more than their share of the weaknesses and foibles of mankind. But their redeeming characteristic is that they always remain interested in themselves; they are fascinated with their human role, and they are filled with the sense that life has a meaning, a meaning which lies just outside their grasp, and that life has truth, a truth that will triumph at last. So, while confronting their weaknesses, wallowing in self-pity, sometimes suffering in silence, and often cursing their bad luck, they surprisingly bounce back from their despair to affirm with Herzog, "but how charming we remain notwithstanding."

The paradox of finding charm in a life fraught with constant anguish and frustrating failures is suggestive of a more central paradox which is implicit in every Bellow novel. It is a paradox which involves the questions, "What are we doing here"? and "Where are we going"? In Bellow's view, man's condition is to be caught between extremes, between the good and the bad, between the beautiful and the ugly, between a state of war and a state of peace, between the finite and the infinite. Man is constantly being pulled in different, opposing directions. To remain a man (or as Bellow has said, "to endure one's humanity"), one must not live at either extreme, no matter how much he might desire or feel driven to do so. For Bellow, the crucial problem confronting contemporary man is how best to adjust to one's "condition," and avoid being pulled to an extreme. How can one achieve some kind of balance between the demands of extreme positions? How does one find the balance between absolute freedom and stifling determination, between love of others and self-pity, between giving and receiving that would enable him to live a life that would be most free from restrictive bonds?

This conflict exists for all of Bellow's protagonists, and whether they relate to it by "becoming neither more nor less than human," by discovering the "axial lines of life," or by achieving a "synthesis" of life's contradictory demands, they are all engaged in a similar quest. Rueben Frank in his essay, "Saul Bellow: The Evolution of a Contemporary Novelist" (1954.B5), was one of the first critics to recognize this quest as a kind of "reserved affirmation," and he

considered Bellow one of the "first of the newer writers who is able
to view tradition, modern wars, and the depression steadily, respect-
fully, and yet face the future unafraid, with hope, seriousness, and
a sense of humor." In 1958 Chester Eisinger (1958.B3) further developed this view in considering Bellow's movement toward a "hedged
affirmation" as seen through heroes who surrender their identity and
then seek to reestablish it. In the first dissertation on Bellow,
"The Crab and the Butterfly: The Themes of Saul Bellow" (1962.A1),
Keith Opdahl discussed this conflict in terms of the competing claims
of a man's will and his love.

Three of the earlier major book-length studies of Bellow deserve
special mention here since they exemplify several other recurring
critical perspectives on Bellow's work: Tony Tanner's Saul Bellow
(1965.A1), Keith Opdahl's The Novels of Saul Bellow (1967.A7), and
John Clayton's Saul Bellow: In Defense of Man (1968.A1).

In the first published book on Bellow, Tony Tanner highly praises
Bellow's work, although he considers that the novels "lack the spine
of a plot, they lack the impact of a sequence of linked incidents."
Such a charge has been leveled frequently against Bellow's novels,
particularly The Adventures of Augie March, and seems to be echoed
by those who, unlike Bellow, tend to place a very high value on
"realistic," cause-effect plots.

Bellow's style has been both praised and damned by critics. While
Tanner finds that his style can be "amazingly vivid and energetic,
graphic in its descriptive force and dazzling in its expression of
thoughts," he believes that it can also be "profligate, uneconomical
and indiscriminate...at times it seems to be straining too hard, trying to create by sheer richness and intensity of language beliefs and
emotions which are not actually there." Bellow himself has admitted
that his style is sometimes effusive and that he occasionally gets
"carried away" while writing; but in his defense many critics have
claimed that if the style in its richness and intensity sometimes
seems false, it is only because the style reflects the characters:
the characters are intense, and they are often struggling for beliefs
and straining to develop emotions which they do not yet possess.

While Tanner criticizes Bellow's weak plots and inappropriate
style, and brings into question his technical ability as a writer,
Keith Opdahl traces the source of a weakness in Bellow to an unre-
solved conflict in his imagination. According to Opdahl, Bellow has
never been able to choose between skepticism and belief, between
willfulness and love. Opdahl believes that this conflict not only
pervades Bellow's style and the structure of his novels, but it also
defines the particular psychological make-up of his protagonists. As
Opdahl views the novels, Bellow's heroes are always faced with the
dichotomy between the demands of their will and the force of their
love, between their natural tendency to be skeptical and their long-
ing for some belief. The central problem for these protagonists is
to reconcile these demands and aspirations. Opdahl further emphasizes

that the only way this reconciliation can come about is through some kind of religious transcendence. But, although he believes that achieving this state of transcendence is the goal of all of Bellow's heroes, Opdahl cannot indicate just what this transcendence involves, since he believes that Bellow himself is not clear on this crucial point.

While Opdahl obviously admires Bellow, he criticizes him for "ambivalence," "indecisiveness," and the lack of a clearly stated philosophical position. Opdahl, like many critics, tends to stress the autobiographical element in Bellow's fiction. He believes that Bellow has never resolved in his own life the dilemmas that his heroes face: Bellow, too, is pulled in different directions, desiring on the one hand to be a man who strongly asserts his will, and, on the other, a man who freely gives of his love.

John Clayton finds the contradictions in Bellow's work and the dichotomy in his imagination to be even more serious than Opdahl finds them to be. Clayton singles out the "desperate" nature of Bellow's affirmation of human dignity. He believes that such an affirmation makes Bellow disavow cultural nihilism while remaining himself a "depressive." Clayton suggests that Bellow participates in and even promotes the nihilism which, in his prose writings, he condemns; there are thus contradictions between the aesthetic Bellow espouses in his non-fictional writing and the quite different views implied in his fiction. Clayton finds, for example, that in his discursive writing Bellow has clearly rejected the tradition of alienation in modern literature, yet all of the major characters in his novels are "alienatees." Furthermore, in his role as critic Bellow asserts how essential it is for man to establish a separate identity and to cultivate a well-developed sense of the self, yet, according to Clayton, his novels deny individuality.

Clayton finds in Bellow a frustrated novelist who is never quite able to practice what he professes. His novels fall short of success because of the unresolvable conflicts and contradictions in his mind; these conflicts create such a crisis in his own imagination that he is unable to project his professed beliefs and attitudes to his characters. Thus, Clayton believes that although Bellow commits himself to a defense of man, he does not know what is to be defended, and, consequently, provides an inadequate, confusing defense.

Clayton's critical approach, like several who have followed him, is to emphasize the contradictions between Bellow's analytical writings and his fiction. But other critics in defense of Bellow believe that this approach ignores the possibility that the contradictions might be apparent because of intentional paradox on Bellow's part rather than because of his confusion as a writer. Bellow's rejection of the tradition of alienation in modern literature does not mean that he must avoid characters who are "alienatees." He has created alienated characters, but in so doing he has not acknowledged the

conclusions of many other contemporary writers whose characters are
also alienated. While many such writers have submitted to the alienation, Bellow resists it. While writing in the same cultural milieu,
Bellow has reached very different conclusions: he is optimistic about
man, even dogmatically so. He maintains optimism because he believes
that there are no viable alternatives; he has said, "Man is all we
have...After nakedness, what"? His position, therefore, is to cling
to hope in spite of the destructive alienation which envelops man.
He asserts his dogma as an act of faith--faith in the possibilities
of love despite the prevalence of hate, faith in the possibilities of
extending oneself to others in spite of the demands of selfishness,
faith in the possibilities of hope despite the opportunities for
despair. His novels are an exploration of the paths by which one
comes to this faith--they are thus quests, quests for the kind of
salvation which is essential in an age when despair afflicts so many
and nihilism has become a prevailing philosophy. In awarding Bellow
the Novel Prize, the Swedish Academy recognized the courageousness of
his position; the Academy stated that his novels are "about a man
without a foothold. But--and this is important--a man who keeps on
trying to find a foothold during his wanderings in a tottering world,
one who can never relinquish his faith that value of life depends on
its dignity, not on its success, and that truth must triumph at last."

General interpretations of Bellow have tended to follow these
lines. Most of the criticism has tended to focus on Bellow's themes,
although his "comedy" has been receiving increasing attention. There
have also been a number of critics who have raised the issue of the
"Jewishness" of Bellow's writing (See Index), an issue which Bellow
himself says is not significant nor highly relevant. Fewer critics
have been concerned with the imagery and symbolism in the novels,
although Bellow's admonition against symbol hunting in his essay
"Deep Readers of the World, Beware!" tended to stimulate a vigorous
symbol hunt in Henderson the Rain King. While each of the novels has
received considerable attention, there has been very little criticism
of the short stories and plays. Despite the large body of secondary
literature already accumulated, much remains to be done.

This bibliography contains annotations of Bellow criticism from
1944 through 1976. Included are reviews and relevant book notices,
general appreciations, bibliographies, biographical sketches, critical
books, collections of essays, chapters in more general books, significant references in books and articles, Ph.D. dissertations, and
several noteworthy M.A. theses. References to some foreign criticism
in French, German, Italian, Japanese, Norwegian, Dutch, Spanish, and
Hebrew have been included, but the selection of foreign criticism is
representative rather than exhaustive. Material which could not be
located for annotation but which was listed in another bibliographical
source has been preceded by an asterisk. The criticism has been
arranged chronologically by year of publication, with each year being
subdivided into two categories, "A. Books" and "B. Shorter Writings."
Arrangement within each of these categories is alphabetical by the

Introduction

last name of the author.   Numbering is sequential within each category; cross-references and index entry numbers are cited by year and section number, e.g., 1944.B3, 1969.A1.   There is one inclusive index with authors, titles, and subjects interfiled.

I wish to acknowledge the help I have received from the work of previous bibliographers as I prepared this reference guide.   Of special note is the earliest bibliography on Bellow by Harold W. Schneider which appeared in Critique (1960.B10).   Also helpful have been the bibliographies by David Galloway (1966.B21) and B. A. Sokoloff and Mark Posner (1971.A2).

I also wish to record my appreciation for the assistance received from the staffs of the California State University, Northridge, library, particularly Mr. Barrett Elcano, and the UCLA Research Library. Professor Walter Graffin, University of Wisconsin, Parkside, has also provided invaluable suggestions and encouragement during the preparation of this book.

Writings about Saul Bellow, 1944-1976

<u>1944 A BOOKS - NONE</u>

<u>1944 B SHORTER WRITINGS</u>

1   ANON. "Introspective Stinker." <u>Time</u>, 43 (8 May), 104.
    Describes <u>Dangling Man</u> as a very carefully written, self-
    pitying novel whose hero is a "pharisaical stinker."

2   CHAMBERLAIN, JOHN. Review of <u>Dangling Man</u>. <u>New York Times</u>
    (25 March), p. 13.
    <u>Dangling Man</u> ventures into unexploited territory, and
    while it is "haphazard in construction and fuzzy in its
    subsidiary characterizations," it significantly brings home
    the ultimate horror of war without getting close to the
    front lines.

3   DeVRIES, PETER. Review of <u>Dangling Man</u>. Chicago <u>Sun Bookweek</u>
    (9 April), p. 3.
    <u>Dangling Man</u> is an excellent first novel which perfectly
    carries out its author's purpose. Bellow clearly under-
    stands the "intracacies of human relationships."

4   FEARING, KENNETH. Review of <u>Dangling Man</u>. <u>New York Times</u>
    <u>Book Review</u>, 49 (26 March), 5, 15.
    <u>Dangling Man</u> is a very imaginative journal in which the
    author "has outlined what must seem to many others as an
    uncannily accurate delineation of themselves."

5   KRISTOL, IRVING. Review of <u>Dangling Man</u>. <u>Politics</u>, 1 (June),
    156.
    <u>Dangling Man</u>, our best war novel, is "superb in its re-
    straint, dignity, and insight." The lean prose is appro-
    priate for the unheroic Joseph who is aimless, hysterical,
    and irritable. The novel operates "on the rock bottom of
    our war-deranged culture."

6   KUPFERBERG, HERBERT. Review of <u>Dangling Man</u>. <u>New York Herald</u>
    <u>Tribune Weekly Book Review</u>, 20 (9 April), 11.

1944

> Bellow's clinical study in <u>Dangling Man</u> requires the tolerance of the reader. Joseph may vaguely symbolize some failing in our modern life, but he leaves the impression of being a "spineless young man," hardly worth the effort of reading about.

7   MAYBERRY, GEORGE. "Reading and Writing." <u>New Republic</u>, 110 (3 April), 473.
> <u>Dangling Man</u> clearly shows that Bellow has an acute ear for conversation. The diary form "has enabled him to present a complex and difficult individial in the round, an event that is rare and wonderful in American writing."

8   ROTHMAN, NATHAN L. "Introducing An Important New Writer." <u>Saturday Review of Literature</u>, 27 (15 April), 27.
> Bellow is original and powerful; he writes "with obvious style and mastery, with a sharp cutting to the quick of language, with a brilliance of thought." One can find "inspired perception" on each of these brief and pungent pages of <u>Dangling Man</u>.

9   SCHORER, MARK. Review of <u>Dangling Man</u>. <u>Kenyon Review</u>, 6 (Summer), 459-61.
> A searching novel with a moral theme, <u>Dangling Man</u> reflects Bellow's interest in psychological and social ramifications. Although it is one of the best books of the year, it is perhaps too unrefined, with the "terms of fiction not wholly achieved."

10   SCHWARTZ, DELMORE. Review of <u>Dangling Man</u>. <u>Partisan Review</u>, 11 (Summer), 348-50.
> <u>Dangling Man</u> is the first novel to capture the experience of a new generation. Joseph's experience is typical; what is not typical is his stubborn confrontation and evaluation of his life. Although the narrative is spare and the journal form limiting, the novel is a significant one.

11   TRILLING, DIANA. Review of <u>Dangling Man</u>. <u>Nation</u>, 158 (15 April), 455.
> Bellow is talented and clever, but his novel is sterile, his characters robbed of human drama and variety. "I demand of pessimism more than of affirmation, that it have a certain grandeur."

12   WILSON, EDMUND. Review of <u>Dangling Man</u>. <u>The New Yorker</u>, 20 (1 April), 78, 81.

Well written and never dull, Dangling Man is "an excellent document on the experience of the non-combatant in time of war." It is "one of the most honest pieces of testimony on the psychology of a whole generation who have grown up during the depression and the war...."

1946 A BOOKS - NONE

1946 B SHORTER WRITINGS

1   HEPPENSTALL, RAYNER. Review of Dangling Man. New Statesman and Nation, 32 (28 December), 488-89.
     A brief review with two other novels. Bellow practices literary nihilism well, and "with a theme that justifies it." Dangling Man is a book filled with "harsh, desperate truthfulness."

1947 A BOOKS - NONE

1947 B SHORTER WRITINGS

1   ANON. Review of Dangling Man. Times Literary Supplement (11 January), p. 21.
     Dangling Man is "neither hard-boiled nor flagrantly romantic." It is rather "an account of an ordinary man's experiences elevated, by imagination, into an individual work of art."

2   ANON. Review of The Victim. The New Yorker, 23 (13 December), 139-40.
     Briefly noted: This novel proves Bellow can go beyond the "subjective broodings" of Dangling Man to tell a fine story "without losing either his sensibility or power." Despite its "poor and ineffectual ending," the novel is an excellent one.

3   ANON. "Suffering for Nothing." Time, 50 (1 December), 111-12.
     The Victim has "troubling depths of meaning which makes it unusual among new novels." This novel is competent, although the final chapter is "out-of-key."

4   CROSS, JESSE E. Review of The Victim. Library Journal, 72 (15 November), 1610.
     Briefly noted: The Victim is "graphically written."

Writings about Saul Bellow, 1944-1976

1947

5   DOWNER, ALAN S. Review of The Victim. New York Times Book
    Review, 52 (30 November), 29.
        It is never clear what the novel is about; it is both
    "overcontrived and undercontrived." Many of Bellow's sym-
    bols and symbolic events are not connected with the actions,
    and we never learn how Leventhal's new found truth frees
    him from Allbee.

6   FARRELLY, JOHN. "Among the Fallen." New Republic, 117
    (8 December), 27-28.
        The Victim confirms Bellow's promise. It is a serious
    but witty book--"witty in the delineation of its characters
    and in the manipulation of its themes."

7   HALE, LIONEL. Review of Dangling Man. Observer (12 January),
    p. 3.
        A brief review, discussed with four other novels.

8   MATCH, RICHARD. "Anti-Semitism Hits a Jew." New York Herald
    Tribune Weekly Book Review, 24 (23 November), 10.
        The Victim is "a subtle and thoughtful contribution" to
    the literature of anti-semitism. Bellow attempts "to com-
    press into the arena the size of two human souls the agony
    of mind which has ravaged millions of Jews in our century."

9   O'BRIEN, KATE. Review of Dangling Man. Spectator, 178
    (3 January), 26.
        Dangling Man is commended with enthusiasm, although it
    is not "holiday entertainment for the casual reader."
    Bellow is a promising author who has taken imaginative
    fiction back "to its true origin, the isolated heart, the
    questioning, separate human soul."

10 POORE, CHARLES. Review of The Victim. New York Times
    (22 November), p. 13.
        A book more disturbing than entertaining, The Victim
    reveals Bellow's skill in exploring a situation to its
    ultimate end. The characters are well-drawn and the sus-
    pense is excellent. The sardonic last chapter suggests
    "that you can never be finally rid of the Kirby Allbees
    of this world."

11 STRAUS, RALPH. Review of Dangling Man. London Sunday Times
    (26 January), p. 3.
        Dangling Man is discussed briefly with four other novels.

1948 A BOOKS - NONE

4

1948 B SHORTER WRITINGS

1 FIEDLER, LESLIE. Review of The Victim. Kenyon Review, 10
      (Summer), 519.
         The Victim is an excellent book, one of the best in ten
      years. Although the ending is disappointing, the novel
      realizes its intent, and it sustains "a tension between
      its realistic surfaces and its symbolic implications."

2 GREENBERG, MARTIN. "Modern Man as Jew." Commentary, 5
      (January), 86-87.
         The Victim is "the first attempt in American literature
      to consider Jewishness not in its singularity, not as a
      constitutive of a special world of experience, but as a
      quality that informs all modern life, as the quality of
      modernity itself." Asa's condition as a Jew is also the
      condition of man in the modern city, a condition charac-
      terized by feelings of being threatened from within and
      without, of not belonging, of not possessing, of having
      trespassed.

3 HALE, LIONEL. Review of The Victim. Observer (13 June),
      p. 3.
         A brief review, comparing The Victim to four other
      novels.

4 HARDWICK, ELIZABETH. Review of The Victim. Partisan Review,
      15 (January), 114-17.
         The Victim is much better than Dangling Man; the writing
      is unpretentious, and the book is more objective. The many
      levels of meaning in the novel arise out of the situations
      in which the characters find themselves.

5 MILLAR, RUBY. Review of The Victim. New English Review, 17
      (July), 89.
         A brief review with three other novels. Bellow is con-
      sidered to be the most promising of recent American novel-
      ists. The Victim is a "penetrating" book in which the
      author "induces an atmosphere of psychological crisis
      which leaves a decided impression upon the mind."

6 SMITH, R. D. Review of The Victim. Spectator, 180 (4 June),
      686, 688.
         A brief review with two other novels. The material in
      The Victim has not been sufficiently ordered, but "the
      characters are so alive, and the range of human feeling so
      extensive," that it is to be commended.

1948

7   STRAUS, RALPH. Review of The Victim. London Sunday Times
        (6 June), p. 3.
            A brief review with three other novels. The Victim
        captures one's interest with its "oddest little story."

8   TRILLING, DIANA. Review of The Victim. Nation, 166
        (3 January), 24-25.
            A much better book than Dangling Man: "Mr. Bellow has
        positively transcended in his second book the self-pitying
        literalness which robbed his first of scale." The book is
        solidly built, "of fine important ideas"; its "physical
        evocations" are impressive, and it can be read on many
        different levels. In not avoiding the delicate sphere of
        interracial relationships, it is "morally one of the far-
        therest reaching books our contemporary culture has
        produced."

1951 A BOOKS - NONE

1951 B SHORTER WRITINGS

1   HOFFMAN, FREDERICK J. The Modern Novel in America: 1900-1950.
        Chicago: Henry Regnery Co., pp. 188-89.
            As a Jewish writer, Bellow is mistrustful of easy opti-
        mism. This is particularly evident in The Victim, where
        Asa Leventhal is "endowed with a talent for applying his
        special form of Jewish analysis to himself."
            Reprinted: 1956.B11; Revised: 1963.B11.

2   WARFEL, HARRY R., ed. American Novelists of Today. New York:
        American Book Co., pp. 32-33.
            A very brief biographical sketch of Bellow.

1952 A BOOKS - NONE

1952 B SHORTER WRITINGS

1   GIBBS, WOLCOTT. Review of a dramatization of The Victim.
        The New Yorker, 28 (10 May), 54.
            Review of a melodrama by Leonard Lesley, based on
        Bellow's The Victim. "There is certainly some material for
        a play in all this, but the writing, the acting, and the
        production...are so inept that nothing emerges except a
        queer confusion."

WRITINGS ABOUT SAUL BELLOW, 1944-1976

1953 A BOOKS - NONE

1953 B SHORTER WRITINGS

1   ANON. Review of The Adventures of Augie March. American
    Scholar, 23 (Winter, 1953-1954), 126.
        A brief paragraph comment: the novel might be sub-
    titled, "Going at Things Free-Style." There are faults of
    construction, but "from now on, any discussion of American
    novelists will have to reckon with Mr. Bellow."

2   ANON. Review of The Adventures of Augie March. Booklist, 50
    (1 September), 1.
        Brief review: "A picaresque twentieth-century adventure
    tale with an amazingly real assortment of characters...."

3   ANON. "Rough Life." Newsweek, 42 (21 September), 102, 104.
        An unfavorable review of The Adventures of Augie March.
    The prose of the novel "consists largely of scrambled
    clichés, dated wisecracks, unfunny jokes, inappropriate
    metaphors, old saws, and political and advertising slo-
    gans...." Despite the facetiousness of the novel, Augie's
    philosophy does give it some significance.

4   ANON. "Some Important Fall Authors Speak for Themselves."
    New York Herald Tribune Book Review, 30 (11 October), 18.
        A compilation of statements by various recently published
    novelists. Bellow's own brief statement indicates why he
    became a writer, and why he also enjoys the role of univer-
    sity teacher.

5   ANON. "What Makes Augie Run?" Time, 62 (21 September), 114,
    117.
        The Adventures of Augie March, "which has a kind of
    self-generating power and authenticity, reads more like
    fictionalized memoirs than a novel." There are some faults
    of style (over-enthusiastic, bloated prose), but the novel
    does push Bellow to the forefront of young American
    novelists.

6   BREIT, HARVEY. "Talk with Saul Bellow." New York Times Book
    Review (20 September), p. 22.
        A biographical sketch of Bellow with particular emphasis
    on the composition of The Adventures of Augie March.
    Bellow stated: "The great pleasure of the book was that it
    came easily. All I had to do was be there with buckets to
    catch it. That's why the form is loose."
        Reprinted: 1956.B6.

1953

7   CASSIDY, T. E. "From Chicago." Commonweal, 58 (2 October),
        636.
            The characterization of The Adventures of Augie March is
        complete "to the point of exhaustion." Many of the charac-
        ters sound like "cheap imitations of Proustians." There is
        no depth and no great theme in the novel; the portraits of
        the old families and their ties and splits "make the book."

8   CONNOLE, JOHN. Review of The Adventures of Augie March.
        America, 90 (31 October), 133-34.
            The novel is unfavorably regarded as "undisciplined,
        amorphous, indefinitely expanded and filled with some of
        the most unpleasant people to appear between the covers of
        a book." Bellow's hero winds up where he starts, as "a
        very foolish and rather incredible young man."

9   CRANE, MILTON. Review of The Adventures of Augie March.
        Chicago Sunday·Tribune Magazine of Books (20 September),
        p. 4.
            Bellow's novel fails to achieve any consistency of tone
        and savor. It is a fragmentary, shapeless series of
        episodes.

10 DAVIS, ROBERT GORHAM. Review of The Adventures of Augie March.
        New York Times Book Review, 58 (20 September), 1, 36.
            Augie is an ideal, detached observer of his own adven-
        tures. Bellow is almost too lavish with the adventures,
        but the complexities of the events keep the novel from
        being cheap or easy. Augie neither finds nor transcends
        himself at the end, but he leaves the reader believing
        that these achievements are now possible.

11 GEISMAR, MAXWELL. Review of The Adventures of Augie March.
        Nation, 177 (14 November), 404.
            The book "pleases everybody and offends nobody," but it
        is not great for "it offers nothing really substantial
        either in the field of human relationships or cultural
        criticism."

12 HICKS, GRANVILLE. "Two New Novels of Life's Mystery." New
        Leader, 36 (21 September), 23-24.
            In this review of The Adventures of Augie March and
        Wright Morris's The Deep Sleep, Hicks finds Bellow's style
        nervous, aggressive, and individualized. Augie, an other-
        directed character, determines to be himself, only he
        doesn't know what he is; the novel details his search to
        find out. "In its language and its ideas, as well as the
        fantastic variety of its cast of characters, it is a

prodigal book, a breathtaking exhibition of sustained
creativity."
Reprinted: 1970.B31.

13   HOBSON, LAURA. "Trade Winds." Saturday Review of Literature,
36 (22 August), 6.
An enthusiastic advance notice of The Adventures of
Augie March with an account of earlier appearances of por-
tions of the book.

14   HUGHES, RILEY. Review of The Adventures of Augie March.
Catholic World, 178 (December), 233-34.
A brief negative review. Although there are some sty-
listic achievements, the novel as a whole has a "fortuitous
air." It is "calculated to achieve more than the sum of
its parts, disparate episodes brought together by the
narrator-protagonist's presence."

15   HUTCHENS, J. K. "On an Author." New York Herald Tribune Book
Review (4 October), p. 2.
A brief profile-interview upon the publication of The
Adventures of Augie March. Bellow's approach to writing
the novel is called "a free swinging, nineteenth century
one." Bellow is grateful for the haven of a university,
but doesn't want to limit his experiences to it.

16   KALB, BERNARD. "The Author." Saturday Review of Literature,
36 (19 September), 13.
A biographical sketch of Bellow accompanying a review of
The Adventures of Augie March. Bellow indicates he had
written 100,000 words of a novel in Paris in 1948, but
discarded it. "Augie was my favorite fantasy. Everytime
I was depressed while writing the grim one, I'd treat my-
self to a fantasy holiday...in Augie one of my greatest
pleasures was in having the ideas taken away from me, as
it were, by the characters. They demanded to have their
own existence."

17   MIZENER, ARTHUR. "Portrait of an American, Chicago Born."
New York Herald Tribune Book Review, 30 (20 September), 2.
The quality of this impressive, successful book comes
"primarily from Mr. Bellow's special sense of the strange-
ness of people." Such a sense produces characters of great
brilliance. The first person narration somewhat limits our
perspective on Augie, and the book would undoubtedly be
better without the cumbersome prose and the "confusing
colloquialisms."

1953

18 PICKREL, PAUL. Review of The Adventures of Augie March.
    Yale Review, 43 (Autumn), x.
        Bellow "substitutes for the meaningful articulation of
    events and characters reportorial fullness." His charac-
    ters, although descriptively interesting, have nothing
    relevant to do. His novel "represents the best and the
    worst in contemporary American fiction--it is both search-
    ing and aimless, both humble and pretentious, both intel-
    ligent and stupid...."

19 PODHORETZ, NORMAN. "The Language of Life." Commentary, 16
    (October), 378-82.
        Bellow, writing "like a man set loose from prison," is
    trying to "put blood into contemporary fiction and break
    through the hidebound conventions of the well-made novel."
    In The Adventures of Augie March, Bellow does not always
    succeed: his prose is too exuberant, his characters one-
    dimensional, his narrative stance confusing. He has not
    yet "worked himself out of the non-dramatic solipsism of
    his earlier books." But his failure is no disgrace; he
    has given us a "sense of what a real American idiom might
    look like."

20 PRESCOTT, ORVILLE. Review of The Adventures of Augie March.
    New York Times (18 September), p. 21.
    Augie is "drunk with the glory of words," and his ideas
    about life and love are somewhat muddled. The novel is
    loose and formless, yet individual episodes are superb and
    the dialogue is often delightful. "...no stranger novel
    has been published in years."

21 ROLO, CHARLES J. "A Rolling Stone." Atlantic, 192 (October),
    86-87.
        The Adventures of Augie March is "the saga of the Amer-
    ican as a rolling stone, an irrepressible explorer who
    doesn't know quite who he is." The novel, while notable,
    does not take us too deeply inside the hero, and comes
    "periously close to being a catalogue of actions."

22 ROSENBERG, DOROTHY. Review of The Adventures of Augie March.
    San Francisco Sunday Chronicle This World Magazine
    (October 25), p. 18.
        This massive novel takes on meaning and direction as
    Augie pursues his inward travels. It is wordy and long,
    yet it includes "some difficult strides into the immeas-
    urable depth that is the soul of every man."

23 WALBRIDGE, EARLE J. Review of The Adventures of Augie March.
    Library Journal, 78 (15 September), 1529-30.
        Brief notice: the novel is "a remarkable, but rather
    exhausting tour de force." It does for Jewish Chicago "what
    James Farrell did for the Irish element there."

24 WARREN, ROBERT PENN. "The Man With No Commitments." New
    Republic, 129 (2 November), 22-23.
        The Adventures of Augie March is a "rich, various, fas-
    cinating, and important book, and from now on any discussion
    of fiction in America in our time will have to take account
    of it." Bellow maintains brilliant narrative pacing within
    the individual incidents, although the novel is somewhat
    uneven with the reason for some of the episodes unclear.
    Augie, a character somewhat static because he has no com-
    mitments, is a "comic version of the modern stoic." In the
    book Bellow displays his own "release of style."

25 WEBSTER, HARVEY CURTIS. "Quest Through the Modern World."
    Saturday Review of Literature, 36 (19 September), 13-14.
        The Adventures of Augie March is a deeply original work,
    making "an apparently complete break with past technique
    and past subject matter." The novel is great "because of
    its comprehensive, not-naturalistic survey of the modern
    world, its wisely inconclusive presentation of its prob-
    lems;...because the style of its telling makes the sequence
    of events seem real even when one knows they couldn't be."

26 WEST, ANTHONY. "A Crash of Symbols." The New Yorker, 29
    (September 26), 128, 130, 133.
        With The Adventures of Augie March, Bellow is aspiring
    for an endorsement from the New Criticism. This "schizoid
    novel" is full of "Melvillean symbols," many of which are
    identified in a parody of New Criticism. The novel focuses
    on the Augie March who has "received bad news from Freud,
    from Marx, and from Dewey," rather than on a living and
    experiencing contemporary man.

27 WEST, RAY B., JR. Review of The Adventures of Augie March.
    Shenandoah, 5 (Winter), 85-90.
        Augie is a character raised to mythic proportions, a new
    version of the all-American boy. Augie's ancestor "is the
    young knight in search of the Holy Grail or rescuing the
    damsel in distress." This being so, the novel does not
    represent a return to the naturalistic novel as has been
    claimed. The novel does arouse genuine expectations as it
    develops, but the "small consolation" Augie is offered at
    the end does little to fulfill them.

Writings about Saul Bellow, 1944-1976

1954

1954 A BOOKS - NONE

1954 B SHORTER WRITINGS

1 AMIS, KINGSLEY. Review of The Adventures of Augie March.
    Spectator, 192 (21 May), 626.
       A brief review with three other novels. The novel is
    important and entertaining, but it is too long and has an
    unfortunate "sentimental vein" in its style. Always behind
    Augie is Bellow, "right in there pitching with his gaiety
    and good humor, his fizzing dialogue, his vitality which
    always rises to the occasion whenever a new character
    appears, his use of learned allusion for burlesque effect,
    and above all his refusal to psychologize or pontificate."

2 ANON. Review of The Adventures of Augie March. London Times
    Literary Supplement (4 June), p. 357.
       Bellow's writing "observes all but interprets nothing."
    The novel, which can be compared with U.S.A. and the Studs
    Lonigan trilogy, is the work of a considerable talent, but
    there is "some obscurity" about Bellow's intentions.

3 COWLEY, MALCOLM. "Naturalism: No Teacup Tragedies," in The
    Literary Situation. New York: Viking, pp. 74-95.
       The Adventures of Augie March is discussed on pages
    91-93. While the novel has subject matter typical of
    naturalistic fiction, it ends as a "personalist" novel,
    affirming the value of a separate person in conflict with
    various social forces.

4 FINN, JAMES. "Notes on Contemporary Novels." Chicago Review,
    8 (Spring-Summer), 104-11.
       Reviewed with several other novels, The Adventures of
    Augie March is found to have a fresh, contemporary idiom.
    The novel reveals "the attempt to achieve a greater inti-
    mation of universality by employing figures from myth,
    legend, and past history for points of comparison."

5 FRANK, RUEBEN. "Saul Bellow: The Evolution of a Contemporary
    Novelist." Western Review, 18 (Winter), 101-12.
       A perceptive survey of the first three novels, this
    essay traces Bellow's move from "tightness and sparsity to
    a free and rich form" and from "despair to a kind of re-
    served affirmation." Bellow's greatest concerns are art
    and morality; in giving voice to the silent generation, he
    is "the first of the newer writers who is able to view tra-
    dition, modern wars, and the depression steadily, respect-
    fully, and yet face the future unafraid, with hope,
    seriousness, and a sense of humor."

12

WRITINGS ABOUT SAUL BELLOW, 1944-1976

6 HARWELL, MEADE. "Picaro from Chicago." Southwest Review, 39
   (Summer), 273-76.
       For the sheer spectacle of people, events, and experi-
   ences, The Adventures of Augie March might best be compared
   to the novels of Thomas Wolfe, although Bellow "stylistically
   sets a keener edge to the literal description of his book, a
   finer temper to the talk." The novel might also be considered "the Renaissance novel now weighed to contemporary action," for Augie reminds one of Panurge in Gargantua and
   Pantagruel. Although the characters are but fragments, the
   plot non-existent and the ultimate meaning of the novel
   vague, Bellow is still the author upon which we can "place
   our finest hopes."

7 HOPKINSON, TOM. Review of The Adventures of Augie March.
   London Magazine, 1 (August), 82-86.
       This brilliant novel appeals to both the reader's sense
   of enjoyment and his judgment. Three weaknesses are apparent: the women are not sharply characterized, Augie's
   philosophical speculations are inappropriately put into the
   "language of vivid reporting," and not all of Augie's
   adventures seem plausible.

8 KRISTOL, IRVING. Review of The Adventures of Augie March.
   Encounter, 3 (July), 74-75.
       Unlike Bellow's earlier novels, The Adventures of Augie
   March "achieves a serenity so pure as to be almost eerie in
   itself." The keynote of the book is "acceptance," and its
   overall effect on the reader is exhilarating.

9 POPKIN, HENRY. "American Comedy." Kenyon Review, 16 (Spring),
   329-34.
       In The Adventures of Augie March, Bellow's vision of the
   great American ambition is comic, not tragic as in many
   earlier American novels. This novel is "strongest when it
   is directly representing Augie's distinctive amalgam of
   aspiration, disaster, and optimism. It is weakest where
   Bellow is furnishing accessories to the main pattern."

10 PRIESTLEY, J. B. "A Novel on the Heroic Scale." London
   Sunday Times (9 May), p. 5.
       The Adventures of Augie March is a tour de force, the
   best new example of the epic-picaresque-comic form "I have
   read in years." The book's force comes from "the unflag-
   ging and astounding zest of Mr. Bellow's narrative." This
   novel is the place to learn about America, for Bellow has
   an extraordinary eye for detail and a great sense of atmos-
   phere. "A triumph."

1954

11 PRITCHETT, V. S. Review of The Adventures of Augie March.
   New Statesman and Nation, N.S. 47 (19 June), 803.
         Reviewed with Isherwood's The World in the Evening.
   Bellow's "rhetoric of the catalogue" is criticized, although
   he is praised for communicating excitement about the city.

12 SCHORER, MARK. "A Book of Yes and No." Hudson Review, 7
   (Spring), 136-41.
         The Adventures of Augie March is an excellent novel,
   although the style and characterization are sometimes un-
   even and shaky. While appearing to be picaresque, the novel
   is not strictly so: its episodes are "confined within a
   thematic, hence a structural pattern." By the end of the
   novel, Augie, the free man, discovers that the value of life
   lies in the living of it.

13 SCHWARTZ, DELMORE. "Adventure in America." Partisan Review,
   21 (January-February), 112-15.
         Superior to other American novels such as Huckleberry
   Finn and U.S.A., The Adventures of Augie March has as its
   theme the satirical acceptance and ironical affirmation of
   experience in America. Augie doesn't want to be prevented
   from having the adventure; hence, his lack of commitment.
   "For the first time in fiction America's social mobility
   has been transformed into a spiritual energy...."

14 WILSON, ANGUS. Review of The Adventures of Augie March.
   Observer (9 May), p. 9.
         Reviewed with two other novels. In utilizing the pica-
   resque, Bellow brings the novel back to its original form.

1955 A BOOKS - NONE

1955 B SHORTER WRITINGS

 *1 DUESBERG, JACQUES C. "Un jeune romancier américain: Saul
    Bellow." Synthesis, 10 (May-June), 149-151.
          Cited in Dommergues, 1967.A3.

  2 KUNITZ, STANLEY J., ed. "Saul Bellow," in Twentieth Century
    Authors, First Supplement. New York: H. W. Wilson Co.,
    pp. 72-73.
          An account of Bellow's career to 1954. Bellow was born,
    July 10, 1915 in Lachine, Quebec, the youngest of four
    children. Bellow himself writes about his early years and
    gives his views on the diminished stature of characters in
    modern novels.

Writings about Saul Bellow, 1944-1976

1956 A BOOKS - NONE

1956 B SHORTER WRITINGS

1   ALDRIDGE, JOHN W. "The Society of Three Novels," in In Search
    of Heresy. New York: McGraw Hill, pp. 126-48.
        Pages 131-39 focus upon The Adventures of Augie March.
    The novel is not a successful adaptation of the picaresque
    form; Augie himself is empty and without commitment.
    Bellow's style is too abstract, and it is "forced to com-
    pensate for the insufficiency of the experience on which it
    is intended to comment."
        Reprinted: 1972.B2.

2   ALPERT, HOLLIS. Review of Seize the Day. Saturday Review, 39
    (24 November), 18, 34.
        Seize the Day is "brilliantly funny, at times profound,
    occasionally exasperating." Tommy has been "compounded
    almost entirely of dilemmas." The other stories in this
    collection are much lesser works.

3   ANON. Review of Seize the Day. Booklist, 53 (1 December),
    174.
        Bellow's writing in this collection is remarkably sensi-
    tive and mature. "The human qualities of the characters
    are revealed most fully in the portrayal of Tommy Wilhelm."

4   ANON. Review of Seize the Day. Time, 68 (19 November), 122.
        In this collection, Bellow suggests that "money is not
    only the root of all evil but also of all plot." The
    stories suffer particularly "from the fact that the leading
    characters are usually the dullest people in them."

5   ANON. "Upper West Side." Newsweek, 48 (19 November), 142-43.
        Seize the Day is a remarkable, although painful, work of
    fiction; it is "masterly in its portraiture and its inten-
    sity of emotion." In Tommy, "the fragility of a human
    being" is thoroughly exposed.

6   BREIT, HARVEY. "Saul Bellow." The Writer Observed. New York:
    World Publishing Co., pp. 271-74.
        Reprint of 1953.B6.

7   CRANE, MILTON. "But Is This One Worth the Telling." Chicago
    Sunday Tribune Magazine of Books (30 December), p. 7.
        Seize the Day is a collection of literal or figurative
    quests in which the seeker is always thwarted. "Bellow
    tells Wilhelm's story expertly enough, but fails to con-
    vince us that there is anything worth the telling."

1956

8   FIEDLER, LESLIE. Review of Seize the Day. The Reporter, 15
(13 December), 45-46.
    In reviewing eight novels published in 1956, Fiedler
finds Seize the Day somber but beautiful: Bellow here re-
turns to his authentic vein, avoiding sentimentality and
the self-destroying irony that marred his earlier works.

9   GOLD, HERBERT. "The Discovered Self." Nation, 183
(17 November), 435-36.
    Seize the Day is undoubtedly "one of the central stories
of our day." Tommy's confrontation with himself helps to
save him in his fragmented society; there is a redeeming
power and a redeeming pleasure in his self-knowledge.

10   HICKS, GRANVILLE. Review of Seize the Day. New Leader, 39
(26 November), 24-25.
    Seize the Day is a novel of economy and strength. It
is a mark of Bellow's achievement that we feel compassion
for Wilhelm and believe in the possibility of his redemption. Wilhelm must learn, though, that he cannot count on
the virtue of others, just as they cannot count on his.
Reprinted: 1970.B31.

11   HOFFMAN, FREDERICK J. The Modern Novel in America. Chicago:
Henry Regnery Co., pp. 188-89.
    Revision of 1951.B1.

12   HOGAN, WILLIAM. Review of Seize the Day. San Francisco
Chronicle (15 November), p. 27.
    Seize the Day is little more than "a vignette of an
American failure." Although this is not his great novel,
Bellow does show himself to be a keen observer of human
frailty and an artist of unusual skill.

13   KAZIN, ALFRED. "In Search of Light." New York Times Book
Review, 61 (18 November), 5, 36.
    Seize the Day is Bellow's "most moving piece of fiction."
His subject is the transparency of human weakness. He is
able to convey to us the world we daily live in, and to
show us that "the real suffering is always the suffering
of not understanding."

14   LYNCH, JOHN. "Prelude to Accomplishment." Commonweal, 65
(30 November), 238-39.
    Seize the Day is a "rather skimpy postscript" to The
Adventures of Augie March, an "interim report," a "fill-in
job."

16

15   PICKREL, PAUL. Review of Seize the Day. Harper's Magazine,
         213 (December), 100.
            The different works in this collection are "united by a
      common concern with what might be called the emotional con-
      vertibility of currency—the way money shapes or displaces
      or disguises the life of feeling."

16   RUGOFF, MILTON. "A Saul Bellow Miscellany." New York Herald
         Tribune Book Review, 33 (18 November), 3.
            The stories in Seize the Day hardly bear comparison to
      the formidable The Adventures of Augie March, but they do
      reveal Bellow's talent. In them Bellow "explores obscure
      emotional patterns, seeking in a variety of ways, many of
      them unorthodox, to convey what goes on within the common-
      place yet strange people he writes about." "The Gonzaga
      Manuscripts" is perhaps the best of the lot.

17   SANAVIO, PIERO. "Il Romanzo di Saul Bellow." Studi Americani,
         2: 261-283.
            In Italian, this essay focuses primarily on The Adven-
      tures of Augie March.

18   SCHWARTZ, EDWARD. "Chronicles of the City." New Republic,
         135 (3 December), 20-21.
            In all of the stories in Seize the Day Bellow "attempts
      to discover pattern and meaning in the hidden fantasies of
      man living in a mechanized urban world where the daily
      routine obscures private realities...." Bellow is seen to
      be like Joyce, and he may be able "to create for America
      the 'uncreated conscience' of modern man."

19   SMITH, T. FRANCIS. Review of Seize the Day. Library Journal,
         81 (1 November), 2584.
            The characters in this collection are forced to come to
      terms with themselves: "the results are disheartening and
      comical but always lifelike."

20   SWADOS, HARVEY. Review of Seize the Day. New York Post
         Weekend Magazine (18 November), p. 11.
            High praise for the stories in this collection which
      are found to be masterful in construction and profoundly
      moving.

1957 A BOOKS - NONE

17

1957

1957 B SHORTER WRITINGS

1 ALLEN, WALTER. Review of Seize the Day. New Statesman and
    Nation, N.S. 53 (27 April), 547-48.
        A brief review with three other novels. Slighter than
    The Adventures of Augie March, this novel has "the same
    acceptance of the contemporary world." What saves Bellow
    is "the energy and firmness of his prose and his astonish-
    ing eye for externals."

2 ANON. Review of Seize the Day. London Times Literary Supple-
    ment (10 May), p. 285.
        This collection shows Bellow's "Dickensian skill in con-
    veying physical presences and actions by an accumulation of
    detail." Bellow's great gifts are particularly shown in
    his excellent characterization of Tamkin.

3 BAKER, ROBERT. Review of Seize the Day. Chicago Review, 11
    (Spring), 107-10.
        The title story of this collection, demonstrating
    Bellow's artistic maturity, "leaves the reader nearly as
    shattered as Wilhelm." While Bellow does not deal con-
    vincingly with women, nor are his novels successfully re-
    solved, his brilliant use of language, his ability to
    portray diverse human experiences, and his success in
    delineating the particularity of the individual make him
    the major talent of the past decade.

4 BAYLEY, JOHN. Review of Seize the Day. Spectator, 198
    (7 June), 758.
        A brief review with four other novels. Bellow, like
    other young American writers, seems "very taken up with the
    question of what it is to be nice." And Tommy Wilhelm
    remains "a real and reverent hymn to niceness, celebrated
    in Mr. Bellow's unemphatically distinguished prose."

5 BERGLER, EDMUND. "Writers of Half-Talent." American Imago,
    14 (Summer), 155-64.
        Bergler examines three novels, including The Adventures
    of Augie March, to support his contention that many poten-
    tially good writers are only writers of half-talent since
    they fail to portray the "unconscious psychic masochism"
    of their heroes. Augie is too passive a character for the
    adventures described, and, if he is a "schizoid-masochistic
    personality," Bellow has incorrectly depicted his emotions.

*6 BOWEN, ROBERT. Review of Seize the Day. Northwest Review, 1 (Spring), 52-56.
　　Cited in Porter, 1974.A3.

7 ELLISON, RALPH. "Society, Morality and the Novel," in The Living Novel. Edited by Granville Hicks. New York: Macmillan, p. 76.
　　Brief mention of The Adventures of Augie March which is "influenced by a knowledge of chaos which would have left the novelists of the twenties discouraged."

8 FENTON, CHARLES A. Review of Seize the Day. Yale Review, 46 (Spring), 452.
　　Displaying Bellow's great wit and range as a writer, Seize the Day is the most exciting in a group of recent American stories. It is "an important book by an increasingly important American writer."

9 FIEDLER, LESLIE A. "Saul Bellow." Prairie Schooner, 31 (Summer), 103-10.
　　It is necessary to come to terms with Bellow, for now, "when the Jews for the first time move into the center of American culture," he stands at the center of American literature as the most prominent Jewish American novelist. Since the Jew is "in the process of being mythicized into the representative American," Augie March has become our mid-century Huck Finn. Bellow's triumphs are triumphs of style (a combination of the intellectual and the informed, the expansive and the tight, the high and the low language, eloquence and slang), and theme (in loneliness one discovers his identity and fellowship with others).
　　Reprinted: 1962.B1; 1964.B31; 1967.A5; 1969.B17.

10 FLINT, R. W. Review of Seize the Day. Partisan Review, 24 (Winter), 139-45.
　　Reviewed with several other novels, Seize the Day is the most "thoroughly achieved" of them all. The title story is a wonderful portrait of upper-Broadway New York; no one since Joyce has rendered the physical city better than Bellow.

11 GILL, BRENDAN. Review of Seize the Day. The New Yorker, 32 (5 January), 69-70.
　　Although Bellow is "among the three or four most talented writers" of the decade, the stories in this collection are not very satisfying because his characters are uninteresting and odious. Bellow "has created a hell of gross, talkative, ill-dressed nonentities, offensive to look at, offensive to listen to, offensive to touch."

1957

12   GLICKSBERG, CHARLES I. "The Theme of Alienation in the Amer-
       ican Jewish Novel." Reconstructionist, 23 (29 November),
       8-23.
           Bellow is considered as a writer who gives a more
       balanced view of the Jew than many other Jewish writers
       (p. 10). In The Victim, Bellow reveals "how each life is
       a microcosmic symbol of all life, how each man carries
       within the seed of all humanity," while also showing with
       compelling sensitivity "the dilemma of a sensitive Jew in
       a hate-ridden world."

13   HOPKINSON, TOM. "Mr. Bellow Disappoints." Observer
       (21 April), p. 11.
           Seize the Day is disappointing after The Adventures of
       Augie March. It is an "uneasy blend of parable and anec-
       dote, with the state of the nation, the state of the world
       as theme." Unfortunately, Bellow is "insufficiently clear
       about his own message, and the end is unconvincing."

14   LOMBARDO, AGOSTINO. "L'arte di Saul Bellow." Realismo e
       Simbolismo: Saggi di Letteratura Americana Contemporanea,
       Biblioteca di Studi Americani, No. 3. Rome: Edizioni di
       Storia e Letteratura, pp. 245-54.
           In Italian, this essay considers both Dangling Man and
       the Adventures of Augie March as examples of the best in
       American writing.

15   ROLO, CHARLES J. "The Human Condition." Atlantic, 199
       (January), 86-87.
           Apart from the unconvincing climax, Seize the Day is
       "sharp and moving." The novella is a study of human weak-
       ness, "striking in its fusion of terrible precision, wryly
       imaginative humor, and compassion."

16   SWAN, MICHAEL. Review of Seize the Day. London Sunday Times
       (21 April), p. 7.
           Tommy Wilhelm is a superbly drawn character, "as crystal
       clear as Gatsby, made to stand eloquently for the neurosis
       that seems to be deep in the plain American man." Although
       Seize the Day is an unsentimental story with a sentimental
       ending, it does reveal Bellow as an artist.

17   WEST, RAY B., JR. "Six Authors in Search of a Hero."
       Sewanee Review, 65 (Summer), 498-508.
           A general review of six recent novels with Seize the Day
       being considered on pages 504-506. This collection was put
       together "more to keep its author's name alive between more
       important projects than as a manifestation of Mr. Bellow at

his best." The theme, unfortunately, represents a return
to Bellow's pre-Augie March period. The hero, Tommy
Wilhelm, is "perversely unheroic" even though the story is
essentially comic.

18 WYNDHAM, FRANCIS. Review of Seize the Day. London Magazine,
    4 (August), 66.
        In a brief review, the novel is praised as being ex-
    tremely well done, even though the final episode "is made
    to bear more significance than it can carry."

1958 A BOOKS - NONE

1958 B SHORTER WRITINGS

1   ANON. Notice of Henderson the Rain King. Booklist, 55
    (15 December), 202.
        Brief advance notice: "An original and compelling novel
    that deals seriously and compassionately with personal re-
    lationships and an individual's search for fulfillment."

2   DAVIS, ROBERT G. "Readers and Writers Face to Face." New
    York Times Book Review, 63 (9 November), 4, 40-41.
        A report on a Columbia University symposium, "The Role
    of the Writer in America," in which Bellow, Wright Morris,
    Leslie Fiedler, and Dorothy Parker discussed and highly
    criticized American writers and their audience. Bellow
    criticized writers who isolated themselves from society,
    thus darkening their vision of life. Writers should be
    more open and communicative, but readers should not expect
    that writers will necessarily create a rich life for them.

3   EISINGER, CHESTER E. "Saul Bellow: Love and Identity."
    Accent, 18 (Summer), 179-203.
        In his novels (through Seize the Day) Bellow has been
    "moving toward a hedged affirmation," revealing again to
    man his greatness, enabling him to complete his life, and
    redeeming him through love. Bellow is concerned with men
    who, at this time in our social history, have lost or
    surrendered their identity and are seeking to regain it in
    themselves and in love. In Dangling Man freedom is the
    condition necessary for self-determination; in The Victim
    responsibility is the key to self-understanding and love;
    in The Adventures of Augie March identity is created
    through experiences which do not completely overwhelm; and
    in Seize the Day one's need must be identified, reclaimed,
    and redeemed.
        Reprinted: 1963.B5.

1958

4   FIEDLER, LESLIE A. "The Breakthrough: The American Jewish
     Novelist and the Fictional Image of the Jew." Midstream,
     4 (Winter), 15-35.
          Pages 34-35 are on Bellow. Bellow is a novelist of
     creative restlessness and adventurousness. His style is
     vigorous, and his constant pursuit is to discover the
     human essence.
          Reprinted: 1963.B6.

5   GEISMAR, MAXWELL. "Saul Bellow: Novelist of the Intellec-
     tuals," in American Moderns: From Rebellion to Conformity.
     New York: Hill and Wang, pp. 210-24.
          The novels through Seize the Day are examined, and
     Bellow is found to be too restricted in his semireligious
     American intellectual view of our modern dilemma. The
     early Saul Bellow "was the Herman Wouk of the academic
     quarterlies," and in his progression as a novelist he has
     been unable to move beyond being oppressed by the moral
     values of his heritage.
          Reprinted: 1967.A5.

6   PODHORETZ, NORMAN. "The New Nihilism and the Novel."
     Partisan Review, 25 (Fall), 576-90.
          Brief mention of The Adventures of Augie March as an
     attempt--one of the last attempts--to assert that indi-
     vidual fulfillment is still possible in our fluid society.

*7   RAES, HUGO. "Amerikaanse Literatuur: Saul Bellow." Vlaamse
     Gids, 42 (December), 283-84.
          Cited in Galloway, 1966.B21.

8   STEVENSON, DAVID L. "Fiction's Unfamiliar Face." Nation,
     187 (1 November), 307-309.
          With the work of Herbert Gold, William Styron, George
     Elliott, Norman Mailer, and Saul Bellow, the novel has
     "undergone a metamorphosis, both in structure and in moral
     assumptions." Their novels "exist in the individual in-
     tensity of a series of moments in the lives of their char-
     acters rather than in a progression of events toward a
     sharply defined denouement." The Adventures of Augie March
     is an obvious example of this.

1959 A BOOKS - NONE

1959 B SHORTER WRITINGS

1   ANON. "A Place in the Sun." London <u>Times Literary Supplement</u>
     (12 June), p. 352.
         After surveying Bellow's earlier novels, the article
     focuses upon <u>Henderson the Rain King</u>, a book "brilliantly
     comic but finally rather unsatisfactory." As an allegory,
     the novel "suffers from Mr. Bellow's double aim of writing
     about man's condition in the world and about moral problems
     specifically American." As a narrative, the first part of
     the book is better than the last part. The novel does show
     Bellow's extraordinary skill "with demotic language."

2   ANON. "A Vocal Group: The Jewish Part in American Letters."
     London <u>Times Literary Supplement</u> (6 November), p. xxxv.
         Part of a special number entitled <u>The American Imagina-</u>
     <u>tion</u>. Bellow is one of the best representatives of "the
     energy of American Jewish writers that has been flowing
     into contemporary letters." He is one of the more extreme
     cases of "the post-war venturesomeness of writers who
     finally have found the social and psychological conditions
     in which they can write boldly as Americans." Bellow has
     taken risks, he has restless daring, and an "unwillingness
     to repeat his material."

3   ANON. "Don Quixote." <u>Time</u>, 73 (23 February), 102.
         In a review of <u>Henderson the Rain King</u>, Henderson's
     ironic adventures are found to "form a highly abstract
     quest for the meaning of life and death, illusion and
     reality, God and man." But he is too Hamlet-like, "too
     greyly overcast with thought." Bellow too often merely
     restates what he ought to develop, and the reader cannot
     tell whether it is "the time that is out of joint or merely
     Henderson's great nose."

4   ANON. Review of <u>Henderson the Rain King</u>. <u>Newsweek</u>, 53
     (23 February), 106.
         A favorable review: In this wild novel, the picaresque
     hero has affinities both to Odysseus and Don Quixote.
     Bellow is a gifted writer and his work exhibits notable
     mastery.

5   BAKER, CARLOS. "To the Dark Continent in Quest of Light."
     <u>New York Times Book Review</u>, 64 (22 February), 4-5.
         <u>Henderson the Rain King</u> is an important, original novel,
     but many readers may be concerned by "the degree to which
     the grotesque and the fantastic have now seized hold upon
     [Bellow's] imagination." The novel looks like "anarchic

1959

romance," which is perhaps not the most sensible form of
conveyance for Bellow's purpose.

6   CAMBON, GLAUCO. "Il nuovo romanzo di Saul Bellow." Aut Aut
    (Milan), 53 (September), 318-20.
    A review of Henderson the Rain King, in Italian.

7   CHASE, RICHARD. "The Adventures of Saul Bellow: Progress of
    a Novelist." Commentary, 27 (April), 326-27, 330.
    Focusing primarily upon Henderson the Rain King, Chase
    also provides a brief analysis of The Adventures of Augie
    March and Seize the Day. Of all of Bellow's novels, only
    in Seize the Day is there "a fully adequate, dramatically
    concentrated image of what the central figure is up
    against--the institutional, family, and personal fate he
    must define himself by, as heroes in the greatest litera-
    ture define themselves." Yet Henderson the Rain King is
    worthy of high praise even though its impact is not con-
    centrated, it falls off in the middle and the imaginative
    Africa isn't an appropriate setting for the hero. "But
    who can complain when, once he is in Africa, we see him in
    episodes which make us think him the momentary equal, for
    tragi-comic madness, for divine insanity, of the greatest
    heroes of comic fiction?"
    Reprinted: 1967.A5.

8   CRUTTWELL, PATRICK. Review of Henderson the Rain King.
    Hudson Review, 12 (Summer), 291-92.
    This novel represents Bellow's attempt to create a
    giant--"a mythic figure, something of the order of
    Rabelais' Gargantua." The giant is America--blundering
    and well-intentioned.

9   CURLEY, THOMAS F. "A Clown Through and Through." Commonweal,
    70 (17 April), 84.
    Henderson the Rain King is a "comedy of suffering" more
    successful than The Adventures of Augie March. Henderson
    is a clown through and through; the entire conception of
    the book is hilarious.

10 DAVIS, ROBERT G. "Salvation in Lions?" Midstream, 5
    (Spring), 101-104.
    Henderson the Rain King is a joy to read, but it does
    not merit much contemplation. Throughout the novel, Bellow
    "is assessing the search for nonrational meaningfulness."
    The symbols don't work, and the experiences of the novel
    cannot be believed. At the end, we still "have the same
    worn-out consciousness which we started with."

11   FRIEDMAN, JOSEPH J. Review of Henderson the Rain King.
      Venture, 3 (Number 3), 71-73.
          This is a profoundly provocative novel, much more com-
      plex and more moiling than Bellow's previous novels. It is
      the brilliant creation of a talented, sensitive and an-
      guished man. The novel is in the genre of fantastic real-
      ism: "there are echoes in it like the growl of thunder
      whose original sound is unheard."

12   GOLD, HERBERT. "Giant of Cosmic Despair." Nation, 188
      (21 February), 169-72.
          Bellow's warning against symbol hunting in Henderson the
      Rain King should be heeded. The novel requires the reader's
      "submission to playful fantasy." But its themes are not
      irrelevant: our religious and philosophical questions never
      remain the same, although our questioning is constant.

13   HARDWICK, ELIZABETH. Review of Henderson the Rain King.
      Partisan Review, 26 (Spring), 299-303.
          This novel is an "autonomous work, a mutation," unlike
      Bellow's earlier novels. Its literal meaning is rather
      thin; "the scenery is too unreal for picaresque comedy, the
      events have too little resonance for symbolic fantasy."

14   HICKS, GRANVILLE. "The Search for Salvation." Saturday
      Review, 42 (21 February), 20.
          Henderson the Rain King is "as exciting a novel as has
      appeared in a long time." Bellow is praised for the clar-
      ity of his theme and for his not indulging in mysticism.
      "The style is the man and Henderson is revealed to us not
      only by what he says but also by the way in which he says
      it."
          Reprinted: 1970.B31.

15   HOGAN, WILLIAM. Review of Henderson the Rain King. San
      Francisco Chronicle (23 February), p. 25.
          This is a thoroughly original novel; the reader should
      not search too deeply for symbolism or he will miss all the
      fun.

16   JACOBSON, DAN. "The Solitariness of Saul Bellow." Spectator,
      202 (22 May), 735.
          This is a favorable review of Henderson the Rain King,
      but with reservations about Bellow as a novelist. Bellow
      has not yet come to terms "with the true nature of his
      talent or genius."

1959

17 KAZIN, ALFRED. "The Alone Generation: A Comment on the Fiction of the Fifties." Harper's, 219 (October), 127-31.
    The writing of The Adventures of Augie March was a liberating experience for Bellow: "he discovered himself equal to the excitement of the American experience, he shook himself all over and let himself go." Bellow in general has a fascination with characters who are "excessive of themselves and their society, insatiable in their demands on life."
    Reprinted: 1962.B3; 1963.B13.

18 _____. "The World of Saul Bellow." The Griffin, 8 (June), 4-9.
    In reviewing Henderson the Rain King for The Readers' Subscription, Kazin discusses the range and significance of Bellow's accomplishment. All of Bellow's heroes are burdened by a speculative quest, and a need to understand their destiny. But beyond this, his novels "offer the deepest commentary I know on the social utopianism of a generation which always presumed that it could pacify life,...but which is painfully learning to celebrate life, to praise in it the divine strength which disposes of man's proposals."
    Reprinted: 1962.B3.

19 KOGAN, HERMAN. "Symbolism Beneath a Rushing Narrative." Chicago Sunday Tribune Magazine of Books (22 February), p. 3.
    Henderson the Rain King is a hypnotic, compelling saga of a person driven to the site of man's origins to seek out the wisdom of man's life and the nature of his destiny.

20 LEHAN, RICHARD. "Existentialism in Recent American Fiction: The Demonic Quest." Texas Studies in Literature and Language, 1 (Summer), 181-202.
    In discussing the influence of Sartre and Camus on Bellow, Ellison, Bowles, and Wright, Lehan finds an "affinity of mind or spirit." Bellow's Joseph has many similarities to Roquentin of Sartre's Nausea and Meursault of Camus' The Stranger. All three are innocent minds coming into contact with the absurd; all three dangle, feel abandoned, and experience the loss of traditional values.
    Reprinted: 1963.B15.

21 LEVINE, PAUL. "Saul Bellow: The Affirmation of the Philosophical Fool." Perspective, 10 (Winter), 163-76.
    The reconciliation of an uncommitted hero to himself and to society is at the heart of Bellow's writing. Joseph remains uncommitted as long as possible in order to define

his commitment and his freedom; Leventhal must accept his responsibilities as a Jew in order to be responsible as a human; Augie examines the commitments of others before understanding his own; and Tommy's quest for identity leads him to accept himself and his guilt.

22   MADDOCKS, MELVIN. Review of Henderson the Rain King. Christian Science Monitor (26 February), p. 11.
While the novel is an interesting, original one, Bellow as a novelist "moves in lunges and plunges."

23   MALCOLM, DONALD. "Rider Haggard Rides Again." The New Yorker, 35 (14 March), 171-73.
An unfavorable review of Henderson the Rain King: the novel is not successful for the hero is "simply too stupid for the task imposed on him." Henderson's statements are "so general as to be meaningless," and he never "betrays the slightest symptom of knowing what he is talking about."

24   MILLER, KARL. "Poet's Novels." Listener, 61 (25 June), 1099-1100.
Brief mention of Henderson the Rain King: it is difficult to know "how seriously or literally we are to take his conversion."

*25   PERROTT, ROY. Review of Henderson the Rain King. Manchester Guardian (29 May), p. 6.
Cited in Book Review Digest, 1959, p. 83.

26   PICKREL, PAUL. "Innocent Voyager." Harper's Magazine, 218 (March), 104.
Henderson the Rain King is much better unified and more brilliantly written than The Adventures of Augie March. Henderson seems to be the "essentially innocent, unfulfilled American, a kind of middle-aged Huck Finn." The novel incorporates a wide variety of themes and situations from earlier American literature.

27   PODHORETZ, NORMAN. Review of Henderson the Rain King. New York Herald Tribune Book Review, 35 (22 February), 3.
This is a novel of "high literary distinction" although curiously unsatisfying. It is "endlessly fertile in invention and idea" and has a grotesque humor that can be compared to Faulkner. Bellow has been able to discipline his virtuosity somewhat; his prose is "charged with all the vigor and virility of colloquial speech and yet capable of the range, precision and delicacy of a heightened formal rhetoric." The author poses great questions in a

1959

psychological and metaphysical context, and perhaps the
weakness of the novel is Bellow's too "heavy reliance on
abstract metaphysical categories."

28   PRESCOTT, ORVILLE. Review of Henderson the Rain King. New
     York Times (23 February), p. 21.
          This "peculiar, prolix and exasperating" novel must be
     considered an unsuccessful experiment, "noble in purpose
     but dismal in result." It cannot be accepted as either
     fantasy or allegory, and, unfortunately, Henderson is not
     an interesting character.

29   PRICE, MARTIN. Review of Henderson the Rain King. Yale
     Review, 48 (Spring), 453-56.
          This is a novel of "originality and unforced invention,"
     having "the concentration, sensuous brilliance, and depth
     of meaning we might expect of a fine poem." Henderson is
     the American Adam; the novel catches "that self-conscious,
     self-indulgent extravagance which seems almost a constant
     in the American idiom...." It is one of the few truly
     American novels of recent years.

30   QUINTON, ANTHONY. "The Adventures of Saul Bellow." London
     Magazine, 6 (December), 55-59.
          Henderson reveals what Bellow's earlier heroes also
     possess: a particular depth and refinement of motivation.
     In Henderson the Rain King Bellow offers yet another of the
     "bewildering variety of forms" that his novels display. Yet
     in his novels there is continuity: through all his tech-
     nical variations, there is "a basic repetoire of human
     character types and of fundamental forms of human
     relationships...."

31   ROLO, CHARLES. Review of Henderson the Rain King. Atlantic,
     203 (March), 88.
          This is an "odd and puzzling" novel. Not essentially a
     parody, the novel seems to be Bellow's attempt to revitalize
     the theme of the search for self-realization. But it is "an
     attempted tour de force which has failed to come off."

32   ROSS, THEODORE J. "Notes on Saul Bellow." Chicago Jewish
     Forum, 18 (Fall), 21-27.
          Although Bellow is considered to be "the most remarkable
     literary talent to emerge on the American Jewish scene,"
     Ross is critical of Bellow's occasional evasiveness and his
     failure "to articulate those realities of social and emo-
     tional experience which he is aiming at." Bellow's empha-
     sis on love and compassion is particularly criticized:

"our author's sometimes wilful stress on these notions appears to be based largely on an undue eagerness...to Christianize the uniquely Jewish experience and uniquely Jewish spirit for the sake of transmitting that unique context into something vaguely acceptable to everybody under the sun."

33 SCOTT, J. D. Review of Henderson the Rain King. London
    Sunday Times (24 May), p. 15.
        A brief review in which the novel is seen as "a half-impressive, half-tiresome book in which the noisy chest-beating prose sometimes illuminates, but sometimes obscures, Mr. Bellow's own visionary glimpses."

34 SOLOTAROFF, THEODORE. "Philip Roth and the Jewish Moralists."
    Chicago Review, 13 (Winter), 87-99.
        Similar to works written by several other recent Jewish novelists, Seize the Day is a "comic action of suffering that leads to the truths of the heart." Bellow shares a preoccupation with "the griefs and potencies" of the heart with Roth and Malamud. As a novelist, Bellow rebels against the position of detachment and impersonality that goes back to Flaubert.

35 STERN, RICHARD G. "Henderson's Bellow." Kenyon Review, 21
    (Autumn), 655-61.
        Henderson the Rain King is a brilliant imaginative construction, a "stylistic masterpiece which stays grounded in the real." The actions of the book are discrete from its ideas; the ideas "exist in terms of Henderson's need." Henderson's reactions to ideas help to reveal his personality.

36 SWADOS, HARVEY. "Bellow's Adventures in Africa." New Leader,
    42 (23 March), 23-24.
        Praises Bellow for celebrating life, and for providing a novel that is intensely pleasurable to read. Especially impressive are the "density and vividness of his descriptive passages, the incredible exuberance of his language and the inexhaustible richness of his imagination."

37 TANASOCA, DONALD. Notice of Henderson the Rain King. Library
    Journal, 84 (1 January), 118.
        Brief notice: Henderson is "an American Gargantua with true Rabelaisian flavor." The reader "will search his memory long for another novel like this."

Writings about Saul Bellow, 1944-1976

1959

38 WAIN, JOHN. "American Allegory." _Observer_ (24 May), p. 21.
    Henderson the Rain King is a moving and true book.
    Africa in this novel is "like the ocean in _Moby Dick_--a
    place where things happen inside a man's soul." The novel
    provides exhilarating reading and continuous excitement.
    Henderson symbolizes America--"Self-discovery, if necessary
    by means of violence and sacrifice: that is the American
    preoccupation. Having discovered their land, they now face
    discovery of themselves."

39 WATERHOUSE, KEITH. "Literary Lions." _New Statesman_, 57
    (6 June), 805-806.
    Henderson the Rain King with its brilliant characteriza-
    tions is Bellow's most powerful novel. Henderson is "about
    half a dozen of civilization's archetypes rolled into one
    rich, bloated, disturbed being...."

40 WEALES, GERALD. Review of _Henderson the Rain King_. _The_
    Reporter, 20 (19 March), 46-47.
    The novel's strength lies in the brilliant, vivid crea-
    tion of the main character: "the incongruity of the man
    and his spiritual needs becomes the heart of the novel that
    is genuinely comic in intention."

41 WHITTEMORE, REED. "Safari Among the Wariri." _New Republic_,
    140 (16 March), 17-18.
    After comparing nine earlier reviews of _Henderson the_
    Rain King (four approved, five disapproved), Whittemore
    joins those who disapprove. It is difficult to become
    involved in the novel; Bellow's parody and his serious
    theme are inconsistent.

42 WILSON, ANGUS. "Books of the Year." _Observer_ (27 December),
    p. 8.
    Brief mention of _Henderson the Rain King_ as "the only
    really important book I have read this year." It is in a
    different class from other fiction (although it had a "too
    conscious desire to be the great American novel.")

1960 A BOOKS - NONE

1960 B SHORTER WRITINGS

1   FIEDLER, LESLIE A. _Love and Death in the American Novel_.
    New York: Stein and Day, pp. 360-61.
    A brief discussion of the lack of "real or vivid female
    characters" in Bellow's work.

Writings about Saul Bellow, 1944-1976

2   FREEDMAN, RALPH. "Saul Bellow: The Illusion of Environment."
    Wisconsin Studies in Contemporary Literature, 1 (Winter),
    50–65.
        In Bellow's novels through Henderson the Rain King, there
    can be found a transformation of the conventional social and
    naturalistic novel; in these novels society reflects "the
    hero's consciousness-functioning as his symbolic mirror--
    while at the same time it also maintains its time honored
    place as the source and creator of his condition." Hero
    and world become related to one another in new ways; real-
    ity becomes evanescent: "In increasingly abstract terms...
    environment as an internal force and as an apparently ex-
    ternal conditioning force imposes itself on his novels
    producing thematic and emblematic motifs."
        Reprinted: 1967.A5.

3   GOLDBERG, GERALD J. "Life's Customer: Augie March."
    Critique, 3 (Summer), 15–27.
        In the elastic, picaresque The Adventures of Augie March,
    Bellow recreates our modern era. The novel is limited,
    however, by Bellow's being "torn between nostalgic re-
    creation of a world he has known and discriminatingly
    writing a cohesive novel." Essentially a passive charac-
    ter, Augie throughout seeks self-knowledge and self dis-
    covery. His quest demands courage and hope; our sympathy
    for him is maintained by the fact that he never adopts the
    cynicism of those around him. Contrasting this novel to
    the earlier picaresque novel, Tom Jones, reveals a sharp
    difference in the moral climate of the two periods, but the
    corruption of our times is not taken by Bellow "as an
    indication of the lessened worth of mankind."

4   HASSAN, IHAB. "Saul Bellow: Five Faces of a Hero."
    Critique, 3 (Summer), 28–36.
        The protagonists of Bellow's first five novels reveal
    "a hero with changing face and steady burden." Each hero
    is discussed in turn; all are found to be "in some way or
    other outsiders to the world they inhabit; all are on in-
    timate terms with pain; and all affirm the sense of human
    life." The progress and development of the hero through
    the novels is from defeat to acceptance to celebration.
        Revised: 1961.B7.

5   HUGHES, DANIEL J. "Reality and the Hero: Lolita and
    Henderson the Rain King." Modern Fiction Studies, 6
    (Winter, 1960–61), 345–64.
        Reading Lolita and Henderson the Rain King in conjunc-
    tion helps throw light on what these books are really about.

1960

Both books "begin with a version of reality that is parodic
and farcical and end with a vision of parody overcome and
farce turned to real anguish and real discovery." Both
novels are quests for reality, and the reader discovers
reality through the heroes' quests. The major weakness of
both novels is that the authors fail to reintegrate their
heroes with society once the quest has been completed.
Reprinted: 1967.A5

6   LEACH, ELSIE. "From Ritual to Romance Again: Henderson the
    Rain King." Western Humanities Review, 14 (Spring),
    223-24.
        Certain elements of plot and situation in the novel
    parallel Weston's From Ritual to Romance, including the
    Grail Quest to restore the Waste Land, the Rain King-
    Medicine Man-Healer, the initiation experience of sleeping
    with the dead, the consequences of not satisfying sexual
    demands, and the continuous, ever-renewing affirmation of
    life.

7   LEVENSON, J. C. "Bellow's Dangling Men." Critique, 3
    (Summer), 3-14.
        Bellow's heroes dangle differently from the typical
    dangling American hero, in part because of the inter-
    national tradition Bellow draws upon. Bellow's own imag-
    ination has been nurtured by American writers and American
    culture, but also by Nietzche, Dostoevski, and Yiddish
    humor. An American writer's problem is to discover whether
    there may not be some new way to be free, or some new turn
    for the imagination to take. In drawing upon the inter-
    national theater of his imagination, Bellow has shown that
    "the American imagination has discovered an old way to be
    free."
        Reprinted: 1967.A5.

8   LEVINE, PAUL. Review of Henderson the Rain King. Georgia
    Review, 14 (Summer), 218-20.
        Involving a quest for both true freedom and true iden-
    tity, this novel has as its theme the "American innocent
    abroad." Although it is not as good a novel as The Adven-
    tures of Augie March, it is original and witty, as well as
    rich and rewarding.

9   MAUD, RALPH. Review of Henderson the Rain King. Audit, 1
    (22 February), 17-18.
        A brief review praising Bellow for grasping "the prob-
    lems of the soul with a firm, human, and humorous hand."

Writings about Saul Bellow, 1944-1976

10 SCHNEIDER, HAROLD W. "Two Bibliographies: Saul Bellow,
    William Styron." Critique, 3 (Summer), 71-91.
        The Bellow bibliography emphasizes fullness, with a
    listing of all relevant pieces and an annotation of the
    most important. Significant or interesting items are
    starred. The material is arranged as follows: (1) Books,
    (2) Short Fiction, (3) Reviews, (4) Articles, (5) Biograph-
    ical Material, (6) Criticism of Bellow's Works.

11 THOMPSON, FRANK H. Review of Henderson the Rain King.
    Prairie Schooner, 34 (Summer), 174-75.
        This novel is a sequel to The Adventures of Augie March,
    for Augie and Henderson are "differing versions of the same
    essential man." Older, Henderson has a greater capacity
    for suffering but still a capacity for change, although the
    change can appear to be madness.

1961 A BOOKS - NONE

1961 B SHORTER WRITINGS

 1 ARNAVON, CYRILLE. "Le roman africain de Saul Bellow:
    Henderson, the Rain King." Etudes Anglaises, 14 (January-
    March), 25-35.
        An essay, in French, focusing upon the structure and
    themes of Henderson the Rain King.

*2 BERGER, YVES. Review of Henderson the Rain King. L'Express,
    No. 523 (22 June).
        Cited in Dommergues, 1967.A3.

 3 DEAKIN, NICHOLAS. Review of Dangling Man. Time and Tide, 42
    (16 March), 435.
        A brief review of a reissue of Dangling Man in England.
    The novel is praised for its "wit and precise observation."

 4 DeMOTT, BENJAMIN. "Jewish Writers in America: A Place in the
    Establishment." Commentary, 31 (February), 127-34.
        In this article about Jewishness and Jewish writers,
    there is high praise for The Victim ("incomparably the
    finest American book about Jewishness"), and Seize the Day
    ("a beautifully detailed, almost flawlessly composed short
    novel"). Enthusiasm for these books is tempered by those
    who seek truth of action, who refuse to believe that "all
    souls are beaten."

1961

5   ESTANG, LUC. Review of Le Faiseur de pluie (Henderson the
     Rain King). Le Figaro littéraire, 794 (8 July), 15.
          In French, high praise for a novel filled with vitality
     and life, one which promises great pleasure in the reading.

6   HASENCLEVER, WALTER. "Grosse Menschen und kleine Wirklichkeit."
     Monat, 13 (February), 71-75.
          A review article, in German, on Henderson the Rain King.

7   HASSAN, IHAB. "Saul Bellow: The Quest and Affirmation of
     Reality," in Radical Innocence. Princeton: Princeton
     University Press, pp. 290-324.
          Revision of 1960.B4.

*8   MEGRET, CHRISTIAN. Review of Henderson the Rain King.
     Carrefour, 882 (9 August).
          Cited in Dommergues, 1967.A3.

*9   PAROT, JEANINE. Review of Henderson the Rain King. Les
     Lettres françaises, No. 881 (22-28 June).
          Cited in Dommergues, 1967.A3.

*10 ROSENTHAL, JEAN. Club du Livre américain, No. 2
     (December 1961-January 1962).
          A general article on Bellow and his works; cited in
     Dommergues, 1967.A3.

11   ROTH, PHILIP. "Writing American Fiction." Commentary, 31
     (March), 223-33.
          Comments on the difficult cultural and political situa-
     tion of today's writers and the effect that this has on
     their style and content. Praises Bellow's style which re-
     flects character. The self should be celebrated by today's
     writers, but not the self when excluded or isolated from
     society.

12   TICK, STANLEY. Review of Henderson the Rain King. Meanjin
     Quarterly, 20 (April), 112-115.
          In a review of several American novels, Tick finds
     Henderson the Rain King "a compelling failure because its
     resolution is obscure." Neither the nature of Henderson's
     affliction nor its cure is readily comprehensible.

1962 A BOOKS

1   OPDAHL, KEITH M. "The Crab and the Butterfly: The Themes of
     Saul Bellow." Ph.D. dissertation, University of Illinois,

193 pp. Listed in Dissertation Abstracts, 22 (April),
3670-3671.
    Examines "the conflict inherent in his (Bellow's) fic-
tion and the psychology central to his characterization."
Bellow frequently juxtaposes the rationalistic man of will
with the joyful man of love; the two character types "reflect the tension in Bellow's art and his attempt to reconcile both realities of the human spirit."

1962 B SHORTER WRITINGS

1   FIEDLER, LESLIE A. "Saul Bellow," in The Modern Critical
    Spectrum. Edited by Gerald J. Goldberg and Nancy M.
    Goldberg. Englewood Cliffs, N. J.: Prentice-Hall,
    pp. 155-61.
        Reprint of 1957.B9.

2   GOLDFINCH, MICHAEL A. "A Journey to the Interior." English
    Studies, 43 (October), 439-43.
        Americans have a tendency to seek symbols and to strive
    after antiquity, spirituality, and rediscovered roots. In
    Henderson the Rain King, Bellow helps us to experience the
    resurrection myth anew in an age when this myth has lost
    much of its meaning.

3   KAZIN, ALFRED. "Saul Bellow," in Contemporaries. Boston:
    Little, Brown, pp. 207-23.
        Pp. 207-17: Reprint of 1959.B17; pp. 217-223: Reprint
    of 1959.B18.

4   KLEIN, MARCUS. "A Discipline of Nobility: Saul Bellow's
    Fiction." Kenyon Review, 24 (Spring), 203-26.
        Traces the movement of Bellow's heroes from a character-
    istic alienation from society to an accommodation with it.
    Also examined is the impact of the city on Bellow's heroes
    and its effect on their personalities.
        Reprinted: 1962.B5; 1963.B14; 1967.A5; 1975.A4.

5   _____. "Saul Bellow," in After Alienation. Cleveland: World
    Publishing Co., pp. 33-70.
        Reprint of 1962.B4.

*6   LEMAIRE, MARCEL. "Some Recent American Novels and Essays."
    Revue des Langues Vivantes, 28 (January-February), 70-78.
        Considers Bellow, Styron, Steinbeck and Pound; cited
    in Galloway, 1966.B21.

1962

7   LEWIS, R. W. B. "Recent Fiction: Picaro and Pilgrim," in
    A Time of Harvest: American Literature 1910-1960. Edited
    by Robert E. Spiller. New York: Hill and Wang, pp. 144-153.
    Considers Augie March to be one of recent fiction's
    picaro-pilgrims. "Part of Bellow's artistic strength comes
    from his cunning fusion of Anglo-American literary tradi-
    tions with Yiddish traditions; and Augie March is what is
    known in Yiddish folklore as schlemazl--that is the comic
    victim of a series of misadventures."

8   LUDWIG, JACK. Recent American Novelists. No. 22, Minneapolis:
    University of Minnesota Press, pp. 7-18.
    A brief consideration of Bellow's novels through
    Henderson the Rain King. Bellow is called the leading
    novelist of his generation, and America's most intellectual
    novelist.

9   MOHRT, MICHEL. "Un enfant de Chicago: Saul Bellow." Le
    Figaro littéraire, 832 (31 March), 2.
    A brief profile of Bellow and his work, in French. While
    often writing of Chicago, Bellow exhibits a humanism far too
    encompassing to be limited to one city, one race, or one
    religion. He is a novelist for all men of today.

10 PRITCHETT, V. S. "That Time and That Wilderness." New
    Statesman (28 September), pp. 405-406.
    Recent American "freeway novelists" such as Bellow,
    Malamud, Mailer and Salinger are contrasted--unfavorably--
    to Faulkner.

*11 RABI. "La Chronique de Rabi." Terre retrouvée (18 February).
    Review of Henderson the Rain King. Cited in Dommergues,
    1967.A3.

12 SWADOS, H. "Certain Jewish Writers," in A Radical's America.
    Boston: Little, Brown, pp. 164-76.
    A brief discussion of the Jewish themes and motifs in
    Bellow's early work.

13 VILLELAUR, ANNE. Review of Au Jour le Jour (Seize the Day).
    Les Lettres françaises, 941 (30 August-5 September), 2.
    While the title story in this collection is not long, it
    can hold its own when compared with the longer works of
    Bellow. Among the shorter works, "Looking for Mr. Green"
    is the most remarkable. In French.

14 WEISS, DANIEL. "Caliban on Prospero: A Psychoanalytic Study
    on the Novel Seize the Day by Saul Bellow." American
    Imago, 19 (Fall), 277-306.

A psychoanalytic study of the father-son relationship in
Seize the Day. The conflict between Tommy and his father
is central to the novel, but "its repressed content is
latent until the very end of the novel when the repression
is shattered." Tommy lives as a victim, a moral masochist;
his aggressions are inhibited or rendered as opposites of
themselves. At the end of the novel, Tommy "gives up his
death wish against the father and accepts...his own role
as victim."
Reprinted: 1967.A5.

1963 A BOOKS - NONE

1963 B SHORTER WRITINGS

1   BRADBURY, MALCOLM. "Saul Bellow and the Naturalist Tradition."
Review of English Literature, 4 (October), 80-92.
In assessing Bellow's novels from Dangling Man to
Henderson the Rain King, Bradbury finds that Bellow's artistic interests link him with the American naturalists and
with Dreiser in particular. Bellow uses the cityscape, and
shows the struggle of urban life; but he also keeps alive
the natural landscape of the spirit and the struggle of the
inner world.

2   _____. "Saul Bellow's The Victim." Critical Quarterly, 5
(Summer), 119-28.
The novel is about man's relationship and responsibility
to the society which makes him, but of which he does not
feel a part; Leventhal's dilemma is thus seen as both a
social and a psychological problem. Leventhal is forced
to develop a sense of obligation to his fellowman, but he
finds that discovering his responsibilities in a competi-
tive and morally confused society is difficult. While
Bellow is indebted to such realists as Dreiser, the styli-
zation of the novel "is all in the direction of mythic and
psychological intensification; the tale becomes a tale for
all men." Bellow's concerns as a writer may thus be compared to those of the French and Russian existentialists.

3   COOK, BRUCE. "Saul Bellow: A Mood of Protest." Perspectives
on Ideas and the Arts (WFMT-Chicago), 12 (February), 46-50.
This interview/profile was written shortly after Bellow
accepted a teaching position at the University of Chicago.
It includes details on Bellow's high school and college
days, and records his opinions on teaching, his role as a
writer, on freedom and friendship, and on the struggle
against evil in life.

WRITINGS ABOUT SAUL BELLOW, 1944-1976

1963

4   DAVIS, ROBERT GORHAM. "The American Individualist Tradition:
    Bellow and Styron," in The Creative Present: Notes on Con-
    temporary American Fiction. Edited by Nona Balakian and
    Charles Simmons. N. Y.: Doubleday and Co., pp. 109-142.
        Discusses each of Bellow's novels through Henderson the
    Rain King in support of the contention that Bellow is very
    conscious of being American and being culturally condi-
    tioned. In his novels Bellow does express our common sense
    of alienation with unusual compassion.

5   EISINGER, CHESTER E. "Saul Bellow: Man Alive, Sustained by
    Love," in Fiction of the Forties. Chicago: University of
    Chicago Press, pp. 341-62.
        Reprint of 1958.B3.

6   FIEDLER, LESLIE A. "The Breakthrough: The American Jewish
    Novelist and the Fictional Image of the Jew," in Recent
    American Fiction: Some Critical Views. Edited by Joseph J.
    Waldmeir. Boston: Houghton-Mifflin, pp. 84-109.
        Reprint of 1958.B4.

7   GALLOWAY, DAVID D. "The Absurd Hero in Contemporary American
    Fiction: The Works of John Updike, William Styron, Saul
    Bellow, and J. D. Salinger." Ph.D. dissertation, Univer-
    sity of Buffalo. Listed in Dissertation Abstracts, 23
    (May), 4356-4357 (Order No. 62-5558).
        The absurd hero, appearing in modern fiction as saint,
    tragic hero, and picaro, is concerned primarily with learn-
    ing how to love. The "absurd sensitivity" doesn't entirely
    account for Bellow's artistic accomplishment, but it does
    help to explain his vision.
        Revised and published: 1966.B21.

8   _____. "An Interview with Saul Bellow." Audit, 3 (Spring),
    19-23.
        An interview conducted at the University of Buffalo in
    December 1962. Bellow answers questions on the "university
    novel," the influence of the academic community on writers,
    the significance of writers of the thirties, the writers
    who have influenced him most, his most satisfying book to
    write, and his expectations for the novel of the future.

9   GEISMAR, MAXWELL. "The Jewish Heritage in Contemporary
    American Fiction." Ramparts, 2 (Autumn), 5-13.
        Serious Jewish writers today have the problem of "which
    Jewish heritage should they hold in their hearts and embody
    in their literary work." After discussing the problem in
    relation to Roth, Salinger, and other Jewish writers,

Geismar focuses upon Bellow ·and Malamud who "belong to the
Partisan Review–Commentary–Dissent axis of literary achievement" rather than to the New Yorker school. Bellow's work
does not seem to be of "the first order of talent"; his
Judaism is "altogether solemn, somber, painridden and joy-
less." His rather orthodox Judaism "is intended as a
retribution for sinning souls and errant spirits."

10   GILMAN, RICHARD. "Novelists in the Theater." Commonweal, 78
        (29 March), 21.
        Reviews the dramatization of Seize the Day by Mary Otis.
     The dramatization was presented by the Theater for Ideas in
     the form of a reading, and was not too successful since
     Bellow's novel "is tightly bound to its own proper form,"
     and Miss Otis "stayed almost entirely faithful to Bellow's
     superb story."

11   HOFFMAN, FREDERICK J. The Modern Novel in America: 1900-1950.
        Gateway edition, Chicago: Henry Regnery Co., pp. 240-43.
        Revision of 1951.B1.

*12 JENSEN, EMILY. "Saul Bellow's The Victim: A View of Modern
        Man." Literature, 4 (1963), 38-44.
        Cited in Galloway, p. 235: 1966.B21.

13   KAZIN, ALFRED. "The Alone Generation," in Recent American
        Fiction. Edited by J. J. Waldmeir. Boston: Houghton
        Mifflin, pp. 18-26.
        Reprint of 1959.B17.

14   KLEIN, MARCUS. "A Discipline of Nobility: Saul Bellow's
        Fiction," in Recent American Fiction. Edited by J. J.
        Waldmeir. Boston: Houghton Mifflin, pp. 121-38.
        Reprint of 1962.B4.

15   LEHAN, RICHARD. "Existentialism in Recent American Fiction:
        The Demonic Quest," in Recent American Fiction. Edited by
        J. J. Waldmeir. Boston: Houghton Mifflin, pp. 63-83.
        Reprint of 1959.B20.

16   MAILER, NORMAN. "Norman Mailer vs. Nine Writers." Esquire,
        60 (July), 63-69.
        In commenting on the novels of nine contemporaries
     (Styron, Jones, Baldwin, Bellow, Heller, Updike, Burroughs,
     Salinger, and Roth), Mailer states that Henderson the Rain
     King may come "the closest to being a great novel." Bellow
     is a curious writer, "with the warmest imagination of any
     writer in my generation." He has a widely cultivated mind,
     but is perhaps "too timid."

1963

17   MAILER, NORMAN. "Some Children of the Goddess." Esquire, 60
      (July), 63-69, 105.
         A brief discussion of Henderson the Rain King. Bellow's
      major weakness is that he creates individuals, but not the
      relations between them.
         Reprinted 1966.B33.

18   RANS, GEOFFREY. "The Novels of Saul Bellow." Review of
      English Literature, 4 (October), 18-30.
         Comments on each of the novels through Henderson the
      Rain King. Bellow is found to be the natural inheritor of
      Melville and Whitman: "He is the most American of all...in
      his conviction that literature matters."

19   STEVENSON, DAVID L. "The Activists." Daedalus, 92 (Spring),
      238-49.
         The new activist hero in the modern novel "remains to
      the end an intrepid opportunist of the self. He is an
      eager, insatiable explorer of his own private experience...."
      Bellow, Roth, and Gold, among contemporary novelists, have
      created this hero most vividly, and The Adventures of Augie
      March represents this fiction at its artistic best. Activ-
      ist fiction has a new concern for the human condition; and
      its heroes must sustain themselves by a commitment to the
      sense of the transient in a cold world which is beyond both
      comedy and tragedy.

1964 A BOOKS - NONE

1964 B SHORTER WRITINGS

1   ALTER, ROBERT. "Heirs of the Tradition," in Rogues' Progress:
      Studies in the Picaresque Novel. Cambridge, Mass.: Harvard
      University Press, pp. 106-32.
         In The Adventures of Augie March, Bellow attempts to
      adopt the picaresque form to the novelistic idiom of the
      mid-twentieth century. Like picaresque heroes, Augie has
      an unquenchable thirst for experience, is a displaced per-
      son, and lives in a "multiverse." But unlike the typical
      picaresque hero, Augie is searching for himself and for
      meaning in his life.

2   _____. "The Stature of Saul Bellow." Midstream, 10
      (December), 3-15.
         Attempts to assess Bellow's achievement as a mid-
      twentieth century writer. Bellow's fiction is viewed as
      "a sustained attempt" to shake off the hypnotic influence

of the great literature of the first half of the century.
Bellow's work demonstrates a "high degree of responsiveness
to the creative innovations of other writers," but his own
literary innovations in all of his novels have been achieved
unobtrusively. Bellow reworks familiar forms and techniques
of the novel--the flashback, the mythic quest, the picaresque, the classically unified novel, and the realistic
novel. Significantly, his heroes retain an innocence, pre-
serving the mystery of being man.
Revised: 1969.B1.

3   ANON. "From Womb to Gloom." Time, 84 (9 October), 92.
A review of The Last Analysis. The play is "all clap-
trap." Bellow has given Sam Levine who plays Bummy "more
bad lines than he can possibly throw away."

4   ANON. "People are Talking About: Saul Bellow, Master Writer."
Vogue, 144 (15 November), 110-11.
A brief profile: Bellow in Herzog "has at last caught
up with his own brilliance." He is now the big American
novelist, "a disciplined craftsman, a creator of characters
that stick in the mind as though written with ink and epoxy."

5   ANON. Review of Herzog. Booklist, 60 (15 July), 1032.
Herzog is a novel "in which isolation and anguish are
not simply written about, but--to an unusually high degree--
actually communicated."

6   ANON. Review of Herzog. Choice, 1 (November), 370.
A brief review: Herzog is an "episodically brilliant
portrait of a Jewish intellectual." The novel's "richness
and density of ideas, philosophies and political comment"
make it an outstanding example of modern American fiction
at its best.

7   ANON. Review of Herzog. Time, 84 (25 September), 105.
Bellow's own potato love may have "damaged the work of
a writer who has long been on the threshold of the U. S.
literary pantheon but has never quite managed the 'big'
novel that would put him there permanently." Although the
new novel is disappointing, and the prose "sometimes
pudding--soft, mushy, and too sweet," individual episodes
are brilliant. But these episodes are not enough: "Bellow
does not seem to be covering any new ground."

8   ANON. Review of The Last Analysis. Newsweek, 64 (12 October),
105.
A brief, unfavorable review: "the play has committed
suicide before its assassination by the producers."

1964

Bellow's intelligence and verbal ability are not manifest
in dramatic terms. The action is forced and incoherent.

9   ANON. Review of The Last Analysis. Saturday Review, 47
    (17 October), 29.
        This is a depressing play, "a futile farcical fiasco."
    Bellow's intentions are not clear; Sam Levine is miscast.

10 ANON. Review of The Last Analysis. Vogue, 144 (15 November),
    64.
        A brief review: A poor production with inconsistent
    acting, "a witty play that was made to seem like a closet
    drama."

11 ANON. "The Altered Heart." Newsweek, 64 (21 September), 114.
        Herzog is the most fully achieved of Bellow's works, a
    milestone in his career. The novel "has the range, depth,
    intensity, verbal brilliance, and imaginative fullness--the
    mind and heart--which we may expect only of a novel that is
    unmistakably destined to last." With this novel, Bellow
    has indicated that he is through with "victim" literature
    and fashionable alienation.

12 BARRETT, WILLIAM. Review of Herzog. Atlantic, 214
    (November), 192, 196.
        Herzog is a web of ambiguities, dangling "at the cross-
    roads between vanished youth and advancing age." The novel
    has no real resolution, but the "unresolved groping gives
    the book even more truth as a chronicle of our time."

13 BOOTH, WAYNE C. "Salvation Justified." Chicago Maroon Liter-
    ary Review (The University of Chicago), 2 (23 October), 1.
        In so good a novel as Herzog, readers need "to come to
    terms with the novel's ideas." While Herzog himself does
    not make his major decisions on the basis of his ideas--
    these decisions "simply arrived"--he does experience threat-
    ening ideas. Herzog's intellectuality is "the best possible
    way for this hero to face the threat of meaninglessness";
    he courageously faces the piercing questions of living in
    an absurd world. Herzog must often put his battle and its
    partial resolution in religious terms, for there is no
    other way to express it: he "is saved because he is not
    damned, which ultimately must mean because his universe is
    not entirely cursed."

14 BOROFF, DAVID. "The Author." Saturday Review, 47
    (19 September), 38-39, 77.
        A biographical sketch of Bellow accompanying a review of
    Herzog. Bellow discusses the production of his play, The

1964

Last Analysis, and comments on Herzog, which went through
fifteen drafts: "I consider Herzog a break from victim
literature. ...in writing Herzog I felt that I was com-
pleting a certain development, coming to the end of a
literary sensibility." An avid reader and a sharp observer,
Bellow can be considered an erudite, professional writer
in the European tradition.

15   BRADBURY, MALCOLM. "Saul Bellow's Henderson the Rain King."
     Listener, 71 (30 January), 187-88.
        Bellow is "one of the most important novelists writing
     in our language to appear since the war." This novel is
     almost a "parody of the romance form," and Henderson's
     final discovery is not without its "deep irony." The novel
     is "an exploration of the possibilities of personal freedom
     in a universe in which many of the constituents are already
     determined."

16   BRADLEY, VAN ALLEN. "A Hero Sick with Abstractions." Chicago
     Daily News Panorama Section (19 September), p. 3.
        Herzog is a kind of universal man; he "plumbs universal
     frailties, universal failures, universal heartbreaks." In
     laying bare the soul of Herzog, Bellow has given us "one of
     the truly searching philosophical performances of our day.
     What is more, it is a bravura performance, rich with learn-
     ing and profundity, dazzling in the grace and lucidity of
     its style."

17   BRAUN, W. Review of Great Jewish Short Stories. Tradition,
     6 (Spring/Summer), 160-62.
        Praises Bellow's selection, and discusses the increased
     interest in Yiddish literature.

18   BRUSTEIN, ROBERT. "Saul Bellow on the Drag Strip." New
     Republic, 151 (24 October), 25-26.
        A review of The Last Analysis which was staged at the
     Belasco Theater in New York. It is potentially a remark-
     able play, with Philip Bummidge "among the most flamboyant
     comic characters ever written for the American stage." But
     the play was poorly cast and poorly staged, resulting in a
     disaster. Although Bellow failed to formulate the play
     sufficiently—the ending is shallow, elements aren't fused,
     the theme isn't fully developed—he did create a "wild,
     anarchic theater piece" that deserved a better production
     than it got.
        Reprinted: 1965.B13.

1964

19   BURNS, RICHARD. Review of Herzog. Library Journal, 89
      (1 September), 3182.
          Brief notice: Herzog is a "magnificent novel" with a
      "singular, brilliant and endearing character."

20   CHAMETSKY, JULES. "Notes on the Assimilation of the American
      Jewish Writer: Abraham Cahan to Saul Bellow." Jahrbuch
      für Amerika-Studien, 9 (1964), 172-80.
          Examines the acculturation, or assimilation into the
      broader stream of American letters, of three generations of
      Jewish-American writers. Bellow is secure in his assimila-
      tion; he writes of the American experience rather than the
      specifically Jewish experience. Yet he does not placate
      the Establishment since he utilizes "the resources and human
      richness inherent in differences."

21   CHEVIGNY, BELL GALE. Review of Herzog. Village Voice
      (8 October), pp. 6, 17.
          Herzog is an "artistically more controlled and intellec-
      tually a tougher book" than The Adventures of Augie March.
      It is a novel about "man's recovery from a miserable sense
      of deprivation." The letters are the most serious vehicle
      of the book's meaning and they serve several important func-
      tions. In the end, Herzog is not saved "by the intellectual
      formulations, nor by what happens to him, but by the resil-
      iency of his unstable character."

22   CLURMAN, HAROLD. Review of The Last Analysis. Nation, 199
      (19 October), 256-57.
          The play is not altogether persuasive; the "analytic
      minutiae" of Bummidge's psyche is too commonplace. Although
      some passages in the play are funny, eloquent and meaningful,
      the production itself had little style, the setting was in-
      appropriate, and the casting poor.
          Reprinted: 1966.B13.

23   CURLEY, THOMAS. "Herzog in Front of a Mirror." Commonweal,
      81 (23 October), 137-39.
          With Herzog, Bellow has written "a comic novel of vigor-
      ous and subtle surface, with dazzling illusions of depth."
      Herzog in the midst of his pain "reveals his own ridicu-
      lousness and brutality and makes us laugh." It is as if
      Herzog is standing in front of a mirror and the reader is
      behind him.

24   DAVENPORT, GUY. Review of Herzog. National Review, 16
      (3 November), 978-79.

Herzog is Leopold Bloom brought up to date. This is
Bellow's best book--bracing for one's character, and admir-
able for its distrust of the self-importance of despair.

25   DOLBIER, MAURICE. "A Lighthouse of Words." New York Herald
      Tribune (21 September), p. 23.
            Herzog, Bellow's best novel, is a "kind of lighthouse,
      which serves the triple purpose of warning, guiding, and
      assuring." It is a "peculiar but sharply flavorful blend
      of eccentricity, wit, tragedy, comedy, travelogue, mono-
      logue, social criticism and philosophical commentary...."

26   DONOGHUE, DENIS. "Commitment and the Dangling Man." Studies:
      An Irish Quarterly Review, 53 (Summer), 174-87.
            Describes the dangling man "type," and the prevalence
      of this type in Bellow's fiction. "...Mr. Bellow's dan-
      gling men seek equilibrium, value, salvation...an earthly
      condition in which the soul may live." They may appear to
      be men of no commitments, but their deepest commitment is
      "to human life itself and to man under the sign of love."
      And they value above all the imagination, and reject that
      in society which is hostile to it.

27   EDELMAN, L. Review of Herzog. Jewish Heritage, 7
      (Winter 1964/65), 3-4.
            In Herzog, Bellow "transmutes the age old essences of
      Yiddishkeit into aching relevancy, the quest of modern man
      for love, goodness, God." Herzog's Jewishness is reflected
      in his strong sense of family, his reflections on childhood,
      his tender-comic vision, and most importantly in his Jewish
      sense of personal responsibility for human history.

28   ELLIOTT, GEORGE P. "Hurtsog, Hairtsog, Heart's Hog?" Nation,
      199 (19 October), 252-54.
            Herzog is a man worth knowing--a man of intellectual
      vigor who can't stop thinking, a man who expresses these
      thoughts in a ceaseless verbal play. Bellow skillfully
      controls his character and the book, maintaining distance
      by carefully juxtaposing comic scenes. Bellow's brilliant
      prose style is one of the chief pleasures of reading the
      book.

*29   ELLMANN, RICHARD. Review of Herzog. Chicago Sun-Times Book-
      week (27 September), p. 1.
            Cited in Porter, p. 202: 1974.A3.

30   FADIMAN, CLIFTON. Review of Herzog. Book-of-the-Month-Club
      News (October), p. 12.

1964

>Some readers will be bored by the novel, but most will
follow Herzog with a kind of "distressed pleasure." "In
few books...is the intellectual as a comic figure developed
with greater inventiveness, insight, and sheer energy."

31   FIEDLER, LESLIE A. "Saul Bellow," in On Contemporary Litera-
      ture. Edited by R. Kostenlanetz. New York: Avon,
      pp. 286-95.
      Reprint of 1957.B9.

32   _____. Waiting for the End. New York: Stein and Day,
      pp. 61-100, passim.
      Bellow is mentioned frequently in a discussion of the
      problems practicing novelists have in confronting the
      modern world.

33   FISHMAN, P. Review of Great Jewish Short Stories. Jewish
      Spectator, 29 (January), 26-27.
      A brief review. This and other similar collections aid
      those who are "interested in playing the game of 'Jewish
      Authors'--and who ask 'Who is a Jewish author and what is
      a Jewish book'?"

34   GALLOWAY, DAVID P. "The Absurd Man as Picaro: The Novels
      of Saul Bellow." Texas Studies in Literature and Language,
      6 (Summer), 226-54.
      Discusses Bellow's first five novels in turn; views each
      of the heroes as a quester in an absurd, pressured world.
      The heroes "all begin their quests with a vision of the
      apparent lack of meaning in the world...but they conclude
      with gestures of affirmation derived to some degree from a
      realization of the significance of love."
      Reprinted with revisions and additions: 1966.B21.

35   GILL, BRENDAN. "Surprised by Joy." The New Yorker, 40
      (3 October), 218, 221, 222.
      Herzog is "...a well-nigh faultless novel" whose dis-
      guised simplicity gives us a kind of aesthetic shock. Un-
      like many critics, Gill believes that "Nobody writes better
      about women than Mr. Bellow...."

36   GORAN, L. "Saul Bellow Makes It to the Top." Chicago Sunday
      Tribune Books Today (20 September), p. 1.
      Herzog is written in the grand style of Tolstoy. This
      novel, from our most important novelist," is a feast of
      language, situations, characters, ironies, and a controlled
      moral intelligence that transcends the fact that we are
      spectators at a hard luck story."

37 GROSS, BEVERLY. "Bellow's Herzog." Chicago Review, 17
     (ii-iii), 217-21.
         The character of Herzog himself matters much more than
     the structure, form, or technique of the novel. The book
     "tries too hard to become a novel at the end," but Herzog
     the man is most interesting when gripped by his obsessions
     and suffering.

38 GUTWILLIG, ROBERT. "Talk with Saul Bellow." New York Times
     Book Review, 69 (20 September), 40-41.
         An informal talk with Bellow at the time of the publica-
     tion of Herzog and the staging of The Last Analysis.
     Bellow indicated he had written 15 drafts of Herzog.

39 HAMILL, PETE. "A Look at Saul Bellow, Writer at the Top."
     New York Herald Tribune (27 September), p. 35.
         A casual conversation with Saul Bellow shortly after the
     success of Herzog had been assured, and while he was pre-
     paring The Last Analysis for production.

40 HANDY, WILLIAM J. "Saul Bellow and the Naturalistic Hero."
     Texas Studies in Literature and Language, 5 (Winter),
     538-45.
         Bellow goes beyond the naturalists' concern with the
     social-economic failures of man, to explore man's moral
     failures, and the state of the human condition in modern
     times. Seize the Day, in particular, provides an image of
     man which enriches "our insight into the human situation."

41 HICKS, GRANVILLE. "Fragile Bits and Pieces of Life."
     Saturday Review, 47 (19 September), 37-38.
         Herzog, unlike Bellow's earlier characters, seeks salva-
     tion by way of the intellect. The book, a difficult one to
     read, can be exciting and challenging, if the reader gives
     himself to it. "Herzog reinforces my conviction that
     Bellow is the leading figure in American fiction today."
     Reprinted: 1970.B31

42 HILL, WILLIAM B. Review of Herzog. America, 111 (28 November),
     718.
         A brief notice. Bellow is one of our most intelligent
     novelists, but Herzog is "undisciplined" with "no effort
     toward decency."

43 HINDUS, MILTON. Review of Herzog. Jewish Frontier, 31
     (December), 11-14.
         Defends Bellow against the charge that he is exploiting
     his Jewish material, but despite this defense, Herzog is

1964

not considered as good a novel as the earlier ones. The
book moves toward a fatalistic sort of existentialism:
"an affirmation of meaningless existence as a Kantian end-
in-itself." Bellow is criticized for being imitative, for
portraying sex as an ultimate value, for worshiping the
charm of children, and for being in "possession of a very
facile and assimilative literary intelligence."

44 HOFFMAN, FREDERICK J. "The Fool of Experience: Saul Bellow's
    Fiction," in Contemporary American Novelists. Edited by
    Harry T. Moore. Carbondale, Ill.: Southern Illinois Uni-
    versity Press, pp. 80-94.
       Examines the different types of protagonists in the
    first five novels as they represent separation, conformity,
    rebellion, or adaptation. The protagonists are united in
    seeking for affirmation. "Bellow has made the move toward
    affirmation a process of some subtlety."

45 HOWE, IRVING. "Odysseus, Flat on His Back." New Republic,
    151 (19 September), 21-26.
       Herzog is a "marvelously animated performance" confirm-
    ing Bellow as a virtuoso of technique and language. The
    novel is remarkable, first-rate; but there is a discrepancy
    between the "dramatic texture and the thematic purpose,"
    and the material seems "puny" in relation to the intended
    theme. Bellow conceived the book "as a stroke against the
    glorification of the sick self," but it turns out to focus
    too greatly on the "thrashings of the sick self."

46 HYMAN, STANLEY EDGAR. "Saul Bellow's Glittering Eye." The
    New Leader, 47 (28 September), 16-17.
       The novel Herzog is autobiographical (though somewhat
    unreliable) in that "Bellow has developed one aspect of
    himself--primarily his guilt and desperation--into a
    character and a story." Bellow's danger in the book is
    garrulousness: "...he has a compulsion to tell all, to
    overtell, to explain all, to explain away." But the novel,
    unified by Herzog's self-analysis and self-discovery, also
    has its beautiful lyric moments.

47 HYMAS, BARRY. "Letter to Bellow." Reconstructionist, 30
    (13 November), 13-15.
       A "letter" to Bellow on the failure of the production of
    The Last Analysis in which the blame is placed largely on
    the director and the producer.

48 KLEIN, MARCUS. "Holy Moses." The Reporter, 31 (22 October),
    53-54.

Like Bellow's other heroes, Herzog is lonely, estranged, and put-upon. But Herzog is even more obsessed with making connections: his adventure is "the rhetoric with which again and again he assaults all dead abstractions, making vital connections between the life of his own person and all universals."

49 KOGAN, HERMAN. "Saul Bellow Talks About His Herzog." Chicago Daily News Panorama Section (26 September), p. 2.
       This column includes Bellow's comments on the writing of Herzog which he prepared for Wings, the review of the Literary Guild Book Club which made the novel one of its monthly selections. Bellow discusses Herzog's pain and his struggle toward order and equilibrium.

50 LAMOTT, KENNETH. Review of Herzog. Show, 4 (December), 80.
       A great deal of the unanimous critical acclaim with which Herzog was greeted seems quite extravagant and even somewhat foolish. Lamott liked the book, but is distressed by reviewers who "are increasingly ready to accept the signs of rejection..., of failure and of emotional imbalance as the stigmata of a sort of modern secular saintliness."

*51 MacGREGOR, MARTHA. Review of Herzog. New York Post (13 September), p. 47.
       Cited in Opdahl, 1967.A7, p. 185.

52 MADDOCKS, MELVIN. "Saul Bellow--New Champ?" Christian Science Monitor (24 September), p. 7.
       Herzog may help to establish Bellow as the "champ" among contemporary novelists. The novel is an important achievement for the hero here rebels against alienation itself, not just against society. It will strike a responsive chord, because the public like Bellow is also disillusioned with disillusionment.

53 MALIN, IRVING. "Herzog, the Jew." Reconstructionist, 30 (16 October), 28-30.
       Prior to Herzog, Bellow's commitment to Jewishness has been ambivalent and obscure. But in this novel, Herzog readily acknowledges his spiritual heritage; the themes are Jewish, and the style of life is Jewish. Herzog and Bellow here accept their "complex fate."

54 MOYNAHAN, JULIAN. "The Way Up from Rock Bottom." New York Times Book Review, 69 (20 September), 1, 41.
       Herzog is the "great payoff book" of the Jewish writers' movement. The book is a masterpiece, an intelligent novel;

1964

its characters are brilliantly drawn. "After Herzog no
writer need pretend in his fiction that his education
stopped in the eighth grade."

*55 NACHMAN, GERALD. "A Talk with Saul Bellow." New York Post
     Magazine (4 October), p. 6.
        Cited in Opdahl, 1967.A7, p. 185.

56 NATHAN, MONIQUE. "Ecrivains juifs d'Amérique." Preuves, 165
    (November), 74-76, 78-80.
        In French, this article on Jewish writers in America
    focuses chiefly on Nathaniel West, Bellow, Malamud, and
    Roth. Bellow is considered one of America's best writers;
    the publication of The Adventures of Augie March, in par-
    ticular, marks an important date in the history of the
    American novel.

57 NATHAN, P. "Rights and Permissions." Publisher's Weekly, 186
    (5 October), 70.
        On the problems success is creating for Bellow: demands
    on his time, speaking requests, decisions about reprints of
    his work, etc. Bellow indicates that Henderson the Rain
    King may even be made into an opera with Leon Kirschner
    composing.

58 PEARCE, RICHARD. "The Walker: Modern American Hero."
    Massachusetts Review, 5 (Summer), 761-64.
        There is a new persona in modern fiction—one who
    "neither escapes society...nor is destroyed by it." This
    new persona is found in the writing of Salinger, Purdy,
    Algren, Mailer, Ellison, and Bellow. Mature heroes like
    Henderson and Augie are concerned with neither "goals nor
    roles" but are in a constant searching state.

59 PICKREL, PAUL. "Testament of a Survivor." Harper's, 229
    (October), 128.
        The prevailing mood of Herzog is a "feeling of the irrel-
    evance of the human." The novel shows the struggle of a
    sensitive, intelligent, imaginative man to keep sane.

60 PODHORETZ, NORMAN. "The Adventures of Saul Bellow," in
    Doings and Undoings. New York: Farrar, Straus, and
    Giroux, pp. 205-27.
        An analysis of the novels, and Bellow's position as a
    novelist, through Henderson the Rain King. Bellow was the
    first gifted American novelist to seek a new, more viable
    orientation to the world of the postwar period. Dangling
    Man signals this with the alienated modern man, Joseph, who

has no revolutionary plan to justify or support his estranged condition. The Victim, which can be considered a
companion piece, attacks the spiritual timidity and prudence
which lies behind the alienation stance. The Adventures of
Augie March reveals a "new Bellow, reborn into exuberance
and affirmation;" such exuberance is tempered by the fright-
ening consequences of the pursuit of success in Seize the
Day, and in Henderson the Rain King Bellow moves further
away from "forced" affirmation. Here, Bellow writes "with
a sharp awareness of the extent to which the problems of
contemporary life are more than merely a matter of individual pathology."

61   PRESCOTT, O. Review of Herzog. New York Times (21 September),
      p. 29.
          Herzog is a brilliant but strange book, "full of confu-
      sions, pretensions, and mannerisms certain to vex some
      readers and to baffle more." Bellow capitulates to liter-
      ary fashion by abolishing "time with a superfluity of flash-
      backs. The book has immense vitality, but is too often
      dull."
          Reprinted: 1964.B62.

62   ____. Review of Herzog. San Francisco Sunday Chronicle:
      This World Magazine (27 September), p. 39.
          Reprint of 1964.B61.

63   PRIDEAUX, TOM. "Don't Let Bellow Get Scared Off." Life, 57
      (30 October), 17.
          Bellow's hero, Herzog, never seems to be in real trouble,
      though he professes to be. It is thus hard to sympathize
      with him; he becomes boring. Bellow should try again.

64   PRITCHETT, V. S. "King Saul." New York Review of Books, 3
      (22 October), 4-5.
          Bellow "seems the only American of this generation to
      convey the feel and detail of urban America, preserving
      what is going on at times when nothing is going on." His
      longer books, like Herzog, are not so good as his shorter
      ones. The theme of Herzog is too general, the personal
      story "unsustaining and banal." But somehow "the novel
      survives and overgrows its own weaknesses," with the best
      things in it being the innumerable "small sketches."
      Bellow's great sense of comedy and his original imagination
      are also evident.

65   RAHV, PHILIP. "Bellow the Brain King." Book Week
      (20 September), pp. 1, 14, 16.

1964

Bellow is America's finest stylist (his style is "sensibility in action"), and the most intelligent novelist of his generation. Herzog, revealing his intellectual mastery, provides remarkable insight into the new and hazardous aspects of modern life. It is the most personal and affirmative of Bellow's novels. His portrait of Ramona is "the modern woman par excellence, who has made good on the sexual revolution."
Reprinted: 1965.B45; 1969.B23.

66 READ, FORREST. "Herzog." Epoch, 14 (Winter), 81-96.
Enthusiastic praise of Herzog; Bellow makes "coherent the biggest chunk of reality since Joyce got his into Ulysses." The novel is built up painstakingly; having elements of many types of novels, it becomes itself a history and synthesis of the novel. "As an anthology of ideas and speculations it even has the quality of being an education."
Reprinted: 1967.A5.

67 SALE, ROGER. Review of Herzog. Hudson Review, 17 (Winter 1964/65), 616-18.
In Herzog, Bellow attempts to set the world right side up, and he seems to have succeeded. Although not without its faults, Herzog is dazzling, "the largest step taken beyond Lawrence and the romanticism that is bought at the terrifying expense of fear and loathing of human kind."

68 SCOTT, NATHAN A. Review of Herzog. Christian Century, 81 (16 December), 1562-63.
Herzog is Bellow's finest achievement, and it shows that Bellow's art has made spiritual progress. Although a "story of salvation and Paradise Regained, Herzog is in no way a solemn morality story." Bellow wants "to convey a most stringent judgment of that Angst-ridden mentality which has for so long been our fashionable mode of 'seriousness,' and he wants to suggest that there is healing in laughter."

69 SIMON, JOHN. Review of The Last Analysis. Hudson Review, 17 (Winter 1964/1965), 556-57.
Although the production of The Last Analysis was poor, the play was provocative and is worth saving. It attempts to understand "what makes life so barely liveable, so little alive." The play has "intense rhetoric that makes the word become flesh before our very ears and eyes."

70 SOLOTAROFF, THEODORE. "Napoleon St. and After." Commentary,
       38 (December), 63-66.
          Herzog is a remarkable book, but by its end the hero
       "hasn't abandoned the old Self but merely found a healing
       illusion of having done so." Bellow has an indulgent flair
       for optimism, but this does not obscure his "incredible
       grasp of the individual human plight."

71 SQUIRRU, RAFAEL. Review of Herzog. Americas, 16 (December),
       34-36.
          In a mock letter to Herzog, Squirru lauds his confes-
       sions, but criticizes him for clinging to "the human."
       There are too many negative aspects of the human to demand
       that one cling to it. One must also strive to go beyond
       himself, beyond his doubts, beyond his structure.

72 STEERS, NINA A. "Successor to Faulkner?" Show, 4
       (September), 36-38.
          Bellow answers the interviewer's questions on his inter-
       est in anthropology, his choice of career, his writing
       habits, writing for the theatre, the value of the novel,
       his identification with his heroes, and the importance of
       vitality in art.

73 TRACHTMAN, PAUL. Review of Herzog. Progressive, 28
       (November), 43.
          Although staggeringly sad, Herzog is "shot through with
       bits of vaudevillian farce." The novel is profoundly
       Jewish in character and flavor, but "no less an American
       saga for that. The Jewish taste for alienation goes hand
       in hand with the old American article, taken over from the
       Calvinists, that the individual should justify himself be-
       fore God. The Puritans once kept journals for that purpose.
       Herzog instead writes unmailed letters."

*74 WAY, BRIAN. "Character and Society in The Adventures of Augie
       March." British Association for American Studies Bulletin,
       8 (June), 36-44.
          Cited in Galloway, 1966.B21.

75 WEINTROUB, BENJAMIN. Review of Herzog. Chicago Jewish Forum,
       23 (Winter, 1964/1965), 163-65.
          Praises Herzog, but is surprised that no letter is
       directed to some "well-known anti-Semite in the United
       States or elsewhere in resentment of the continuous perse-
       cution and the agony of the Jew." Bellow provides no final
       answers to Herzog's travail, but, given our contemporary
       period, this is "artistically correct."

1965

1   TANNER, TONY. <u>Saul Bellow</u>. Writers and Critics Series.
    Edinburgh: Oliver and Boyd, 120 pp; American edition:
    New York, Barnes and Noble. Bibliography.
        The first published book on Bellow. Following an intro-
    ductory chapter in which he discusses Bellow's background,
    the sources of his inspiration, and some of his ideas on
    self and society, Tanner devotes a chapter to each of the
    novels through <u>Herzog</u>. <u>Dangling Man</u> is found to be some-
    what crude, but with engaging, serious themes. <u>The Victim</u>,
    although weak in its ending and in the analysis of some
    motivations, does effectively probe the problem of what the
    self owes the self and what the self owes the rest of the
    world. <u>Augie March</u> is particularly noteworthy for Augie's
    voice, which "with its wide-ranging delight and wondering
    openness to experience, does justify the move towards wis-
    dom and affirmation." <u>Seize the Day</u> emphasizes that the
    deeply entangled business of life and the world's business
    are very different; and the uncertain <u>Henderson</u> "reaches
    away from negation toward celebration." <u>Herzog</u>, Bellow's
    best, "seems to be the result of a conclusive grappling
    with the gathering preoccupations of years." All in all,
    Bellow refuses a negative stance, and has been constantly
    moving toward the joy of affirmation.
        Extract appears in 1965.B57.

1   ALLEN, WALTER. "War and Post-War American," in <u>The Modern</u>
    <u>Novel in Britain and the United States</u>. New York:
    E. P. Dutton, pp. 321-332.
        Bellow's novels through <u>Henderson the Rain King</u> are
    briefly considered. Although Bellow is considered to be
    "one of the richest and most exciting talents in contem-
    porary writing," he as yet has divisions in himself (intro-
    vert vs. extrovert) that must be resolved. "Affirmation
    is not necessarily the more convincing for being made in a
    stentorian voice."

2   ANON. "Man Who Would be Marvelous." <u>Times Literary Supple-</u>
    <u>ment</u> (4 February), p. 81.
        A review of <u>Herzog</u>: Herzog asks himself "most of the
    fundamental questions which a modern American might ask,"
    answering some of them at length, with irony and illumina-
    tion. The novel is a "big, untidy and sometimes difficult
    book" with "enough ideas and themes for a dozen lesser
    novels."

3   ANON. Review of Herzog. Virginia Quarterly Review, 41
       (Winter), ix.
            Herzog is another Bloom, but one who is searching for
       himself. The author "contents himself with simple exposi-
       tion, never resolution" and it is hoped that he will some-
       day discover "themes complex and subtle enough and of
       sufficient consequence to match his own superb resources."

4   ANON. Review of The Last Analysis. Booklist, 61 (15 April),
       777.
            Brief review: Bellow's "preoccupation with the ultimate
       meaning of existence edges even the most raucous and irrev-
       erent scenes of a play that carries its emotional weight
       with ease."

5   ANON. Review of The Last Analysis. Choice, 2 (September),
       400.
            Brief review of revised version of script: Bellow has
       "not yet mastered the stage." The play should not be pro-
       duced, but should be read to enjoy Bellow's rich imagination.

6   BAILEY, JAMES W. Review of Herzog. Social Education, 29
       (January), 49-50.
            Herzog is a demanding, but immensely rewarding book. It
       does not fail to recognize our world's limitations, but nei-
       ther does it ignore the possibilities. It suggests "we are
       under a spell of ideas, but that ideas have no real signif-
       icance unless we can establish vital human connections."

7   BATTAGLIA, FRANK. Review of Herzog. San Francisco Chronicle:
       This World Magazine (7 March), p. 43.
            Herzog is a novel which belies the widespread belief
       that the modern novel is an affirmation of helplessness.
       Herzog discovers resources within himself to prevail de-
       spite the modern dilemma of meaninglessness.

8   BAUMBACH, JONATHAN. "The Double Vision: The Victim by Saul
       Bellow," in The Landscape of Nightmare. New York: New
       York University Press, pp. 35-54.
            The Victim is one of our most important nightmare novels
       in which man is confronted with his own distorted image.
       Allbee serving as Leventhal's antagonist and double also
       becomes unwittingly the means to his redemption. The novel
       reveals Bellow's debt to both Dostoevsky and Kafka.

9   BERNSTEIN, MELVIN H. "Jewishness, Judaism, and the American
       Jewish Novelist." Chicago Jewish Forum, 23 (Summer),
       275-82.

1965

> After considering several Jewish novels and novelists,
> Bernstein focuses upon Herzog. "Herzog's mind is the Jew-
> ish mind historically at home in all civilizations but re-
> jecting the anti-Jewish, the non-Jewish, those values that
> do not affirm empirical and transcendental Judaistic values."
> The novel can be considered "the American Jewish novel, the
> culmination of the immigrant novel of fifty years ago, with
> Jewishness here meaning not sociology but values."

10   BIENEN, LEIGH. "Literature and National Identity in New
     American Fiction." Transition (Kampala, Uganda), 5
     (No. 20), 46-51.
> Of the novels under review, Herzog offers the best exam-
> ple of "the oblique way in which national identity is ex-
> pressed, and created, in fiction." In the character of
> Herzog, Bellow defines both society and the individual.
> Herzog's "thought and despair about the country are so
> clearly felt and acted, they become moving." His views of
> American society are "completely believable because they
> are backed up by a physical creation of that society, its
> buildings, its habits, its way of talking to itself."

11   BRADBURY, MALCOLM. "Saul Bellow's Herzog." The Critical
     Quarterly, 7 (Autumn), 269-78.
> Herzog offers one of "the fullest and most explored pre-
> sentations of modern experience we have." Of all Bellow's
> novels, Herzog best balances the conflicting claims on the
> individual, while providing a wide ranging debate. The
> novel is an attempt "to define in the context of the
> twentieth-century egalitarian democracy, and twentieth-
> century political and psychological thought, just what
> man's definition of his own humanity may consist of."
> Bellow rejects the morbid, cynical, self-pitying definition
> of man.

12   _____. "Self Against the Mass." Punch, 248 (27 January), 145.
> Herzog is an excellent novel that deserves its acclaim.
> "One of Bellow's great gifts is that of locating experience
> in its social and historical context." The level of dis-
> course in Herzog is metaphysical: "His characters speak
> and think freely of their souls and ask questions about the
> stature and nature of man."

13   BRUSTEIN, R. S. "Saul Bellow on the Dragstrip," in Seasons of
     Discontent. New York: Simon and Schuster, pp. 172-75.
> Reprint of 1964.B18.

14   CAPON, ROBERT F. "Herzog and the Passion." _America_, 112
       (27 March), 425-27.
          Bellow, as a Jewish writer, accurately and marvelously
       paints in Herzog the present condition of man. This is a
       picture of man far fairer than most Christians could draw.

15   COLEMAN, JOHN. "Bellow at his Blackest." _Observer_
       (12 September), p. 26.
          A brief review of _The Victim_ with two other novels.
       Bellow's great power is in establishing environments. This
       novel implies "that life itself is really the victim; that
       all of us are at the mercy of one another's fears and the
       blind forays of chance." It is "as serious and substantial
       novel about the relationship of man alone with man in
       society...as any I know of."

16   COREN, ALAN. Review of _The Victim_. _Punch_, 249 (27 October),
       624.
          Unlike the state of some of Bellow's later heroes,
       "there is nothing mystical about Leventhal's alienation;
       his is no search for salvation, no hunger for a transcen-
       dental truth or meaning." Magnificent and deeply moving,
       the novel is as involved "with the threat of urban exis-
       tence, as with the perpetual pressure upon the Jew in a
       potentially alien society."

17   CORKE, HILARY. Review of _The Victim_. _Listener_, 74
       (16 September), 429.
          A brief review: the characters are very real, and their
       dialectic is "relevant, contemporary, eternal."

18   CORRIGAN, R. W. Review of _The Last Analysis_. _Book Week_
       (23 May), p. 4.
          The publication of this play is a major event; in it
       Bellow attempts to "lead the theatre to those frontiers
       beyond absurdity." Even though the production was a fail-
       ure, the play itself is significant. It reveals Bellow's
       strategy for dealing with the absurd: one must allow the
       actor in himself to emerge and to play all of life's
       roles--"to act furiously within the paradoxes of life in
       order to cope with our consciousness of its absurd terms."
       Philip Bummidge is a modern day Hamlet, "leavened with a
       liberal dose of the Quixotic."

19   CROZIER, ROBERT D. "Themes in _Augie March_." _Critique_, 7
       (Spring-Summer), 18-32.
          Using Jacques Maritain's concept of theme, Crozier dis-
       cusses the theme complex in _The Adventures of Augie March_;

it is a pentagonal pattern, "characterized by an objectifi-
cation of action, character, and comment in centers of reflection upon character-fate, power, money, love, and
urbanization." Bellow deals largely with supra-psychological
poetic values, and thus the novel is "not realistic in the
sense of earlier picaresque or more recent naturalism."

20 [ENCK, JOHN.] "Saul Bellow: An Interview." <u>Wisconsin
    Studies in Contemporary Literature</u>, 6 (Summer), 156-60.
        An interview conducted on April 24, 1964. Bellow an-
    swers questions on the influence of Europeans on American
    writers, on creative writing courses, on contemporary writ-
    ers, on modern criticism, editors, and the life of the
    writer.

21 FINKELSTEIN, SIDNEY. "Lost Social Conventions and Existen-
    tialism: Arthur Miller and Saul Bellow," in <u>Existentialism
    and Alienation in American Literature</u>. New York: Inter-
    national Publishers, 252-69.
        In Bellow's <u>Herzog</u>, the process of existentialist self-
    analysis becomes the finished work. The self-analysis
    leads Herzog to the view that the world is absurd and he
    must protect himself from this absurdity while laughing
    at it. Bellow, as the "self-appointed clown of the Ameri-
    can existentialist movement," develops a similar motif in
    his other works.

22 FRONCEK, TOM. Review of <u>Herzog</u>. London <u>Tablet</u> (6 February),
    p. 154.
        <u>Herzog</u> is a brilliant novel which will acquire "a per-
    manent niche in American literary history." Bellow con-
    stantly undercuts Herzog's pedantry and egotism with comedy
    and affectionate mockery." His artistic skill is also seen
    in "his manipulation of time and memory to tie his philo-
    sophical and sociological themes intimately to his
    characters."

23 GALLOWAY, DAVID D. "Clown and Saint: The Hero in Current
    American Fiction." <u>Critique</u>, 7 (Spring-Summer), 46-65.
        Henderson is considered one of the clowns of contemporary
    American fiction, a recipient rather than an instigator of
    action, an ineffectual buffoon who suffers from bad timing.
    Upon leaving Africa, Henderson abandons the role of the
    clown, moving from "a comical becoming to a being which
    exalts the human spirit."

24 GARD, ROGER. "Saul Bellow." <u>Delta</u>, 36 (Summer), 27-30.
        In <u>Herzog</u> Bellow has the interest of the philosopher
    rather than the novelist, and it makes us wonder just what

kind of novel it is. Unfortunately, Bellow is more interested in the implications of Herzog's actions, than the
actions themselves.

25   GARRETT, GEORGE. "To Do Right in a Bad World: Saul Bellow's
     Herzog." The Hollins Critic, 2 (April), 1-12.
          Ostensibly, this is a review article on Herzog, but it
     turns out to be an appreciation of Bellow--his themes, his
     craftsmanship, his brilliance. "Bellow's career as a writer
     ought to be a joy to anyone who cares about writing.
     ...enjoy the spectacle. It's not likely to happen again
     for a century."

26   GREENBERG, A. D. "The Novel of Disintegration: A Study of a
     World View in Contemporary Fiction." Ph.D. dissertation,
     University of Washington, 295 pp. Listed in Dissertation
     Abstracts, 25 (March), 5278 (Order No. 65-1874).
          Bellow is considered with other contemporary novelists
     of disintegration (Celine, Beckett, Robbe-Grillet, West,
     Algren, Malamud, and Ellison) because of his concern with
     the process of a disintegrating world. The novel of dis-
     integration is studied from the aspects of point of view,
     structure, process, and choice.

27   GROSS, JOHN. "Duel in the Sun." Encounter, 25 (July), 64-65.
          A brief article describing the wrangling, dithering, and
     the political machinations that went on at the Prix
     Formentor conference in St. Raphael, France, before Bellow
     was awarded the $10,000 prize for Herzog.

28   GUTTMAN, ALLEN. "Bellow's Henderson." Critique, 7
     (Spring-Summer), 33-42.
          Henderson the Rain King shows the movement of Henderson
     from one verb (want) to two others (imagine, love), and
     in the final scene of the novel Bellow dramatizes the love
     and imagination. Although he longs for Being, Henderson
     learns to accept himself as one of the Becoming people.

29   HARPER, HOWARD MORRALL, JR. "Concepts of Human Destiny in
     Five American Novelists: Bellow, Salinger, Mailer, Baldwin,
     Updike." Ph.D. dissertation, Pennsylvania State University.
     Listed in Dissertation Abstracts, 25 (May), 6625-26
     (Order No. 65-4380).
          In considering human destiny, Bellow has moved in an
     existential direction. For him, the inner interpretation
     of life matters most. His heroes "move away from tradi-
     tional, systematic and restrictive views of man toward a
     full acceptance of the existential human condition."

1965

30   ISSAC, DAN. "Orpheus Transcending." Judaism, 14 (Winter),
     125-27.
         A strongly positive review of Herzog which emphasizes
     Herzog's quest and his comic sense of life. "...Bellow's
     book achieves existential dimension by always allowing
     Herzog's ideas to grow out of the personal events and in-
     tricate emotions of his life."

31   KAZIN, ALFRED. "My Friend Saul Bellow." Atlantic, 215
     (January), 51-54.
         An informal portrait of Bellow and a brief review of
     Herzog. Several years before Bellow's first novel was
     published, Kazin found him to have a dramatic sense of
     destiny, a writer "pledged to grapple with unseen powers."
     As a man, Bellow is patient yet eager, serious yet sardonic,
     intellectual but not contemptuous. As a novelist, his most
     striking quality is "his ability to make the reader see
     dramatic new issues in situations that a great many people
     live with." In Herzog, Bellow projects his image of life:
     always a "confrontation of opposites, a marriage of un-
     likely possibilities."

32   KERMODE, FRANK. Review of Herzog. New Statesman, 69
     (5 February), 200-201.
         Bellow is one of the best American novelists and Herzog
     supports this position. "...why should we be surprised
     that Americans make much of such powers of invention and
     intellect, such comic energy, so genuine a speculative
     quest?"

33   KUEHN, ROBERT E. "Fiction Chronicle." Wisconsin Studies in
     Contemporary Literature, 6 (Summer), 132-33.
         Herzog reminds one of the great tradition of the novel,
     but it never achieves its philosophical aim of joining the
     personal and the historical in a single drama. The novel
     lacks "a firm design, a coherent and significant story."

34   LAMONT, ROSETTE. "The Confessions of Moses Herzog." Massa-
     chusetts Review, 6 (Spring/Summer), 630-35.
         A private book such as Herzog is popular because of its
     sincerity and "the long frustrated curiosity of the peeping
     toms of the literary world." Herzog longs for contact, for
     serious communion; "the mock communion of letter writing
     parodies mystical union and provides a key" to the book.
     Reprinted: 1966.B31.

35   LEMON, LEE T. Review of Herzog. Prairie Schooner, 39
     (Summer), 161-62.

Herzog--non-depraved, non-diseased, not unlucky--somehow interests us, even though he is so unspectacular. The reason is that Bellow has created a character whose greatest gift is vitality, one who can both think and feel simultaneously.

36 LOMBARDO, AGOSTINO. "La narrativa di Saul Bellow." Studi Americani (Roma), 11 (1965), 309-44.
      A novel by novel analysis, in Italian, of Bellow's works through Herzog.

37 LUDWIG, JACK. "The Wayward Reader." Holiday, 37 (February), 16-19.
      Herzog is a superbly intricate book, a "major break-through." In the contradictions of Herzog's life, Bellow presents the contraditions of the modern world. In Herzog he combines the victim comically with the imposter, the suffering joker. With Bellow, the novel form is "in good hands."

38 MALIN, IRVING. Jews and Americans. Carbondale, Ill.: Southern Illinois University Press, pp. 73-75, 97-98.
      The writings of Bellow, and six other writers who deal with the Jew in America, are mentioned as expressions of a Jewish heritage and Jewish traditions. Themes of exile, fathers and sons, time, head and heart, and transcendence are discussed, as well as the techniques of irony and fantasy.

39 _____. "Saul Bellow." London Magazine, 4 (January), 43-54.
      Examines two recurring tensions in Bellow's work: "madness versus sanity" and "prophecy versus preaching." The madness of society and the self, with its components of narcissism, abstractionism, and compulsion, must be encountered and, hopefully, counteracted by each of the heroes. In the early novels the madness is gothic; in the later novels it is humorous. Bellow's "prophetic style" captures the mad action of his heroes.

40 MATHIS, J. C. "The Themes of 'Seize the Day.'" Critique, 7 (Spring/Summer), 43-45.
      Explores the significance of the title in the narrative development of Seize the Day. Wilhelm learns to seize the day, not by Tamkin's example, but by recognizing the community of man and by giving expression to the compassion and love of his true soul.

1965

41   MILLER, KARL. "Leventhal." New Statesman, 70 (10 September),
     360-61.
          Leventhal is a more ordinary kind of hero than Bellow's
     others, and thus the general reader might more easily relate
     to him. The Victim is "Bellow's most rewarding novel, and
     a novel of great quality." The facts of the relationship
     between Allbee and Leventhal must be understood; there is
     no need "to pry for some higher significance." The limits
     of their relationship are clear, although other elements in
     the book are not clear--such as the psychopathology of
     Leventhal and the "therapeutic satisfactions provided by
     Allbee's revenge."

42   MOHRT, MICHEL. "Saul Bellow et son roman Hertzog." Le Monde
     (8 May), p. 12.
          A general estimate of Bellow as a novelist, and a brief
     review of Herzog, following Bellow's receipt of the Prix
     International de Littérature.

43   MUGGERIDGE, MALCOLM. Review of Herzog. Esquire, 63 (January),
     24.
          Herzog is only "nominally fiction" with a strongly auto-
     biographical flavor. While the hero is a "sniveling, hope-
     less sort of man," the novel is written with an exceptional
     "richness of style."

44   POIRIER, RICHARD. "Bellows to Herzog." Partisan Review, 32
     (Spring), 264-71.
          An "unsufferably smug" book, Herzog is highly overrated.
     Herzog and the author are constantly being confused. There
     is no indication that Bellow is aware of "the essential
     irrelevance, and the essential pretensions and shabbiness
     of the self-aggrandizing mind at work in, and for, the
     hero."
          Reprinted: 1975.A4.

45   RAHV, PHILIP. "Saul Bellow's Progress." The Myth and the
     Powerhouse. New York: Farrar, Straus, and Giroux,
     pp. 218-24.
          Reprint of 1964.B65.

46   RAINES, CHARLES. "The Writer and the Common World." Library
     Journal, 90 (1 April), 1622.
          Critical of Bellow's National Book Award Acceptance
     Speech for Herzog, Raines finds Bellow at fault for criti-
     cizing today's imaginative writers as specialists and
     rebels.

47   RIBALOW, HAROLD. "The Woes of Herzog." Congress Bi-Weekly,
         32 (18 January), 14.
         Herzog is both impressive and dull; it is a "lengthy and
      awkward character portrait of a Jewish intellectual" by a
      writer who doesn't know how to tell a story.

48   RICHLER, MORDECAI. "Number One." Spectator (1 October),
         p. 425.
         Notice of a re-issue of The Victim, a remarkable novel
      about "WASPS going to seed and Jewish guilt."

49   _____. "The Survivor." Spectator (29 January), p. 139.
         An enthusiastic review of an enriching novel: Herzog
      is a "brilliant revelation of character," filled with "in-
      cident and marvelous intentions, zany characters and mem-
      orable dialogue." It is a major work that can "easily
      support all the American praise that has been heaped upon
      it." Bellow is the most gifted of American novelists for
      he writes of life as it really is, without sham or pretense.

50   ROSE, W. K. "The Suffering Joker." Shenandoah, 16 (Winter),
         55-58.
         Herzog marks a broadening of scope for Bellow, with a
      professional intellectual as a hero. The use of letters is
      a brilliant technique to survey the human condition from
      every angle. The novel can be placed beside the epics of
      Melville and Joyce; among novels in English of this cen-
      tury, only Ulysses "is comparable in intellectual scope."

51   ROTHCHILD, SYLVIA. "Commitment to Non-Commitment: A 'Jewish'
         Novel." Conservative Judaism, 19 (Summer), 49-52.
         Herzog is a brilliant novel, but the "zest, excitement
      and affirmation...exist only in Saul Bellow's style, not in
      the substance of the novel." The novel is "both true and
      false, sensitively artistic and mawkishly sentimental, full
      of ideas and yet anti-intellectual. As a 'Jewish' novel,
      it is flawed by its acceptance of the experience of Jewish
      life while denying the meaning of that experience."

52   ROVIT, EARL. "Bellow in Occupancy." American Scholar, 34
         (Spring), 292-98.
         Herzog is a comic novel of ideas, skillfully written
      with multiple perspectives and several layers of irony.
      While not rising to the heights of Faulkner and Hemingway,
      Bellow is our most important novelist, one who is "desper-
      ately honest in trying to face up to the soul-crushing
      intellectual challenges of our time."
         Reprinted: 1967.A5.

1965

53 RUBENSTEIN, RICHARD. "The Philosophy of Saul Bellow."
    Reconstructionist, 30 (22 January), 7-12.
        Herzog's world is exclusively Jewish, and he accepts
    himself as a Jew. His salvation "consists in accepting the
    givenness of his present with its instabilities and the
    fixity of his past with its failures and sorrows." In
    showing how Herzog arrives at a new starting point in his
    life, Rubenstein analyzes his relationship with Madeleine,
    Ramona, Gersbach, and his psychoanalyst.

54 SAPORTA, MARC. "Un Roman d'Anti-Amour: Herzog de Saul Bellow."
    Preuves, 177 (November), 88-89.
        Novels of passion and love have been conspicuously absent
    in the best of American literature. This article, in French,
    notes the rise of anti-love novels in the United States, the
    most conspicuous recent example of which is Bellow's Herzog.

55 SPENDER, STEPHEN. "Bellow in Search of Himself," in The Great
    Ideas Today. Edited by Mortimer Adler. Chicago: Ency-
    clopaedia Britanica, Inc., pp. 170-173.
        Herzog is distinguished by the intensity of his con-
    sciousness that he is an instrument through which the world
    is experienced. The novel realizes the total subjectivity
    of Herzog, and while this is its special achievement, it is
    also its weakness: the novel doesn't provide a point of
    view from which we can see Herzog objectively. "Herzog is
    subject; all the other characters are object." But apart
    from this the novel is remarkable: it "exists within a
    language, packed, textured, and rich, with which Bellow can
    do anything he likes."

56 STEINER, GEORGE. "Moses Breaks the Tablets." London Sunday
    Times (31 January), p. 48.
        High praise for Herzog--a novel "grim and hilarious,
    rambling and beautifully knit, sensuous and actively intel-
    ligent." Although the book is a monologue, it is marked
    by a "sheer prodigality of insight, of humour, of exact
    sensuous rendition so great that it makes most of current
    fiction look shoddy and mannered."

57 TANNER, TONY. "Saul Bellow: The Flight from Monologue."
    Encounter, 24 (February), 58-70.
        The two characters in Bellow's earliest fiction, "Two
    Morning Monologues," are almost archetypes for his later
    work: the "withdrawing, denying, dangling man" and the
    "dodging, weaving, risking man." Henderson represents the
    latter; Herzog the former. Herzog is the "silent mono-
    loguist par excellence." All of Bellow's characters seem

to find "the inner world of spirit more real than the outer
conditioned public world." For this reason, his characters
seldom initiate action and his books lack the spine of plot.
Nonetheless Bellow is the most important American post-war
novelist for his "sheer intelligence," his "firm grasp of
many of the central problems, concerns, and paradoxes of
modern urban thinking man, his matchless feeling for cities,"
"...and his refusal to relinquish a sense of possible individual worth."
Excerpted from 1965.A1.

58   TOYNBEE, PHILIP. "The Odyssey of Herzog." Observer
     (31 January), p. 26.
         Bellow's conclusions about our times and about our indi-
     vidual natures are of real importance. As a novelist, he
     is brilliant, but he never quite pulls together his
     "Dickensian zest for description" with his deep understand-
     ing of the general state of man's mind and spirit in this
     century. In Herzog the "urgent central theme is often dif-
     fused and weakened by all the social and nostalgic
     decoration."

59   TREVOR, WILLIAM. Review of Herzog. The Listener, 73
     (4 February), 201.
         Herzog is a literary accomplishment. "...its application
     is universal, and its nice balance of tragedy and comic
     episodes is a masterpiece of construction."

60   WEBB, W. L. Review of Herzog. Manchester Guardian Weekly,
     92 (4 February), 10.
         Herzog is not a faultless work, but it is rich, com-
     plicated, and very beautiful. It is a courageous novel--
     "courageous not just in the scale and difficult form of the
     general assault which Bellow mounts on the problems of
     modern consciousness, but in the resolution with which he
     offers his own griefs and strivings." Here is the "voice
     of a man letting out all the truth he knows about himself."

61   WINEGARTEN, R. "Victim of Alternatives." Jewish Observer and
     Middle East Review, 14 (15 October), 21-22.
         The Victim is "one of the most disconcerting novels of
     the post-war period." The theme of anti-Jewish prejudice
     is only a point of departure, a pretext for exploring the
     secret self. "Bellow is really more deeply concerned with
     those 'craters of the spirit' to which all may be drawn,
     regardless of origin and condition."

1965

62 YOUNG, JAMES DEAN. "Bellow's View of the Heart." Critique, 7 (Spring/Summer), 5-17.
Examines the structural relations in Herzog--the narrative action, the theme, the point of view, and the narrative focus. These structural relations are what make the novel unique and valuable; sociological, psychological, philosophical, or autobiographical considerations may be important in responding to the novel, but it is the form that gives the novel its unique significance.

63 ZINNES, HARRIET. Review of Herzog. Books Abroad, 39 (Autumn), 460.
Bellow's technique has "surrealistic overtones." The novelist "seems to write out of some kind of affirmation. In this tragicomedy, the final solution does not seem credible, but does it matter?"

1966 A BOOKS

1 DUTTON, ROBERT F. "The Subangelic Vision of Saul Bellow: A Study of His First Six Novels, 1944-64." Ph.D. dissertation, University of the Pacific. Listed in Dissertation Abstracts, 27 (5: November), 1363A (Order No. 66-10, 941).
Bellow's view of man's nature as "subangelic" allows for an existence of dignity and integrity in spite of the vicissitudes of the human condition. This study shows how each of the novels (through Herzog) exalts man's nature, and confirms Bellow's position within the humanist tradition.

1966 B SHORTER WRITINGS

1 ALDRIDGE, JOHN W. "Nothing Left to Do but Think--Saul Bellow," in Time to Murder and Create. New York: David McKay Co., pp. 87-94.
Bellow's work is the "intellectual literature" that many intellectuals have been waiting for. Bellow and Mary McCarthy are the only two American writers who come close to producing an intellectual fiction "that speaks with some real urgency and intimacy to intellectuals."

2 _____. "The Complacency of Herzog," in Time to Murder and Create. New York: David McKay Co., pp. 133-38.
Herzog "deals expertly with materials which most of our novelists have found immensely difficult to dramatize, the materials of consciousness itself, and it deals with them in such a way that we recognize them to be central to our experience, uniquely expressive of ourselves and our

condition as intellectuals." Although Herzog does become complacent, he does provide the most flattering image of the intellectual to be found in modern literature. The ideas of the novel are not offensive or arguable, and it is "as wholesome and nutritious as a dish of cornflakes." Reprinted: 1967.A5; 1972.B2.

3 ANON. "Profiles of American Authors: Saul Bellow." English Teaching Forum, 4 (Autumn), 21-24.
A profile of Bellow, hailing him as the finest stylist and most intelligent novelist of his generation. Some details of Bellow's early life are given, but primary focus is on the themes of the novels through Herzog.

4 ANON. Review of Under the Weather. Saturday Review, 49 (12 November), 34.
Unsatisfying, although not uninteresting, these three comic playlets provide "three memorable scenes, each of which could be an effective part of a longer part but none of which really stands by itself."

5 ANON. "Science and the Clown." Times Literary Supplement (31 March), p. 261.
The Last Analysis, rewritten after its Broadway flop, deserves another chance in the theatre. Bummidge, the main character, is "entirely a creature of the author's irony." The play is witty with brilliant characterization and a "well-sustained level of intellectual farce."

6 ANON. "Sex as Punishment." Time, 88 (4 November), 85.
In the three plays comprising Under the Weather, the relations between the sexes are more painful than pleasurable. Although Bellow's language is witty and literate, he has not learned "that language is not the master of the stage but simply a fuse to ignite dramatic action."

7 BINNI, FRANCESCO. "Percorso Narrativo di Saul Bellow." Il Ponte, 22 (June), 831-42.
In Italian, this essay deals with the range and significance of Bellow's fiction.

*8 BLOCH-MICHEL, JEAN. Review of Herzog. Nouvel Observateur (9 December).
Cited in Dommergues: 1967.A3.

9 BURGESS, ANTHONY. "The Jew as American." Spectator (7 October), pp. 455-56.
A notice of the reprinting of Bellow's novels (Dangling Man through Herzog) by Penguin Books. In his more mature

1966

work "Bellow has opted for the delineation of a complex dis-
satisfied personality, a heaving centre with a periphery
glittering with near-hallucinatory detail." Bellow makes
the American Jew the spokesman for all Americans, but he
does not play up Jewishness or Jewish themes sensationally.
His creations are vital, his language rich.

*10   CABAU, JACQUES. Review of Herzog. Express (20 November).
       Cited in Dommergues, 1967.A3.

11   CASTY, ALAN. "Post-Loverly Love: A Comparative Report."
       Antioch Review, 26 (Fall), 399-411.
         Saul Bellow's Herzog, Arthur Miller's After the Fall,
and Federico Fellini's 8½ all share a sophisticated, penetrating version of the general quest-for-love theme. The
heroes share a similar plight, similar difficulties in
coming to terms with their childhood, and similar difficulties in perception. Awareness of the complexity of love
by heroes in all three works has been ennervating and dis-
abling. Herzog's "return to life" is stimulated by a new
understanding of his childhood, a reaffirmation of living,
and a renewed ability to feel love.

12   CLURMAN, HAROLD. Review of Under the Weather. Nation, 203
       (14 November), 523-24.
         These three one-act plays are something from "the lighter
side of Bellow's talent." They are unpretentious, suggest-
ing "a writer of complex talent still insecure in handling
a medium to which he is not accustomed."

13   _____. "The Last Analysis," in The Naked Image. New York:
       Macmillan, pp. 44-47.
       Reprint of 1964.B22.

14   COREN, ALAN. "Displaced Persons." Punch, 251 (19 October),
       603.
         A review of The Penguin Saul Bellow, the novels Dangling
Man through Herzog. The action in Bellow's novels is "the
treadmill of self-inquiry; the heroes are incapable of
actions which might save them from their own anguished
souls." What universalizes Bellow's heroes is "the ter-
rible fact that, as each day passes, displacement, disorientation, insecurity, fear, suspicion, are ceasing to
be the specific agonies of one race, and becoming the
agonies of all."

15   DETWEILER, ROBERT. "Patterns of Rebirth in Henderson the
       Rain King." Modern Fiction Studies, 12 (Winter, 1966/67),
       405-14.

Henderson the Rain King's artistic design "employs the
context of fantasy to create and sustain the moral concern."
The rebirth concept, in particular, frequently recurs in
the novel and carries the redemption theme. Four devices
by which Bellow develops this theme are identified and discussed: (1) the animal imagery which reveals Hendersons's
transformation from a lower to a higher creature; (2) symbols of psychological reality which describe rebirth in a
Freudian-Jungian context; (3) variations of the hero myth
and the myth of the dying king; and (4) an irony which
directs the ultimate meaning of the book toward the paradox
of redemption.

16   DICKSTEIN, MORRIS. "For Art's Sake." Partisan Review, 33
     (Fall), 617-21.
         Bellow, in his long-standing feud with the New York
     literati, ignores the value of criticism and the place of
     the critic. Criticism often implements the changes in
     human sensibility that great art effects.

17   DOMMERGUES, PIERRE. Review of Herzog. Le Monde (30 October),
     p. 17.
         Herzog is highly praised as a rich, complex, and intrigu-
     ing novel.

*18 _____. Review of Herzog. Magazine littéraire (28 November).
     Cited in Dommergues, 1967.A3.

19   FOSSUM, ROBERT H. "The Devil and Saul Bellow." Comparative
     Literature Studies, 3 (1966), 197-206.
         Although not a "religious" writer, Bellow does reveal in
     his novels a concern with matters of the spirit and the
     state of man's soul. His heroes discover the reality of
     Good and Evil. The essay describes how the protagonists--
     Joseph, Leventhal, Augie, Wilhelm, and Herzog--come to un-
     derstand depravity, a depravity which would "rob man of his
     soul, the essence of his being, and then turn him into an
     object, something to be manipulated...."
     Reprinted: 1967.B12.

20   GALLOWAY, DAVID D. "Moses-Bloom-Herzog: Bellow's Everyman."
     Southern Review, 2 (Winter), 61-76.
         In Herzog Bellow unites various earlier themes and de-
     vices including his characterization of the impotent victim
     and the comic, instinctual rebel. A thematic and stylistic
     source for the novel could be Joyce's Ulysses: Moses E.
     Herzog can be considered a "collatoral descendent...of
     Joyce's Herzog-Bloom." Like the quests of other Bellow

1966

heroes, Herzog's quest for salvation is resolved when he realizes "that man's triumph comes when he has learned to sustain the vital equilibrium between reality and intention." Reprinted: 1966.B21.

21 GALLOWAY, DAVID D. "The Absurd Man as Picaro," in The Absurd Hero in American Fiction: Updike, Styron, Bellow, Salinger. Austin: University of Texas Press, pp. 82-139.
    Each of Bellow's novels through Herzog are examined to reveal a "band of questing men who dissipate their powers and energies in fruitless, often comic quests for salvation...."
    Revised, with new preface and updated bibliographies in 1970.

22 GILMAN, RICHARD. "Bellow on Broadway." Newsweek, 68 (7 November), 96.
    An unfavorable review of the three plays, Under the Weather. Bellow falls short, and his intelligence as a novelist has gone to waste. Shelley Winters is miscast, the production is folksy, and the play should have been produced off Broadway, for commercial theatre can't depart from its "notions of what is comic."

23 GREENBERG, ALVIN. "The Death of the Psyche: A Way to the Self in the Contemporary Novel." Criticism, 8 (Winter), 1-18.
    Brief reference to Henderson the Rain King, pp. 11-13. Henderson's character comes into existence and is revealed through the phenomenal realm, not the psychological. The way in which he moves in his world reveals the meaning of his existence.

24 HARPER, GORDON L. "Art of Fiction: Saul Bellow, An Interview." Interview No. 36. Paris Review, 9 (Winter), 48-73.
    An important interview conducted during September and October of 1965 at the University of Chicago. Harper describes the setting for the interview in some detail. Bellow devoted considerable time to preparing for the interview and revising some of the original material, for it "had become an opportunity, as he put it, to say some things which were very important but which weren't being said." Bellow responds to questions on the literary tradition of which he feels a part, on realism, on literary influences and interests, on the lifting of restraints in the writing of The Adventures of Augie March, the changed style in Henderson the Rain King and Herzog, the "primitive commentator" within him, his preparations for writing, and on the

popularity of Herzog. He also comments on the rhetoric of
writing, the use of comedy, the environments of his novels,
the radicalism of some writers, the distractions of a
writer, and ideas in the novel (especially in Herzog), and
the novel of ideas.
Reprinted: 1967.B14; 1975.A4.

25 HASSAN, IHAB H. "Quest and Affirmation in Henderson the Rain
King," in The Modern American Novel. Edited by M. R.
Westbrook. New York: Random House, pp. 316-324.
Reprinted from Hassan, 1961.B7.

26 _____. Radical Innocence: Studies in the Contemporary Novel.
New York: Harper and Row, pp. 290-324 on Bellow.
Revised edition of Hassan, 1961.B7.

27 HUX, SAMUEL H. "American Myth and Existential Vision: The
Indigenous Existentialism of Mailer, Bellow, Styron, and
Ellison." Ph.D. dissertation, University of Connecticut,
340 pp. Listed in Dissertation Abstracts, 26 (9: March),
5437 (Order No. 66-857).
The existentialism of Bellow derives as much from
nineteenth-century American literature as it does from the
European Existentialists. Such existentialism is comic
rather than tragic, "announcing a faith in still existing
but yet unexplored possibilities for the desperate
protagonist."

28 JONES, D. A. N. "What About the Workers?" New Statesman, 71
(3 June), 819-20.
A review of The Last Analysis and three one-act plays
published with it: "Orange Soufflé," "The Wen," and "Out
from Under." The Last Analysis is a play about "the American predicament as seen by university teachers...." The
three one-acters provide a good evening at the theater,
although the audience winds up feeling themselves "somehow
superior to the characters on stage."

29 JOTTERAND, FRANCK. "Herzog? Une Comédie." La Quinzaine
littéraire (15-30 November), p. 11.
A conversation with Bellow, in French, during which
Bellow answers questions on his comic creations,the culture-
explosion in the United States, the effects of success, his
own style, and the character of Herzog.

30 KAZIN, ALFRED. "Imagination and the Age." Reporter, 34
(5 May), 32-35.

1966

Kazin reviews the talents, the imaginations, and the good books of the forties and fifties before focusing on Mailer and Bellow. He believes that Bellow's "crisis mentality" accounts for much of his popularity. But Bellow's greatest appeal is his ability to command language. Language is salvation; for most writers today it has become "their conscious hope, their feeling, their only known means of transcendence."

31 LAMONT, ROSETTE. "The Confessions of Moses Herzog." Langues Modernes, 60 (September-October), 116-20.
A review of Herzog, in English, focusing upon Herzog's movement toward contact and communication. Lamont accounts for the popularity of the novel, in part, because of "the long frustrated curiosity of the peeping toms of the literary world."
Reprint of 1965.B34.

32 LAS VERGNAS, RAYMOND. Review of Herzog. Les Nouvelles littéraires (29 December), p. 5.
This review, in French, considers the novel substantial, but not one of Bellow's best. Herzog's constant suffering becomes monotonous.

33 MAILER, NORMAN. Cannibals and Christians. New York: Dial Press, pp. 104-130.
Reprint of 1963.B17.

34 _____. "Modes and Mutations: Quick Comments on the Modern American Novel." Commentary, 41 (March), 37-40.
Herzog, unlike heroes of earlier American novels, is "passive, timid, other-directed, pathetic, up to the nostrils in anguish." Herzog as a character is over-educated, dull, and inept. Yet he arouses our compassion and the novel succeeds. He is at the center of the modern American dilemma: mediocrity inspires love.

35 McCARTEN, JOHN. "Look, Ma, I'm Playwriting." The New Yorker, 42 (5 November), 127-28.
An unfavorable review of the stage production of Under the Weather. Bellow "might be happier writing scripts for underground movies than trying to create plays without submitting to the discipline of the theatre." The plays are thin, the characters dull.

36 MUDRICK, MARVIN. "Who Killed Herzog? or Three American Novelists." University of Denver Quarterly, 1 (Spring), 61-97.

Bellow, along with Malamud and Roth, has taken upon himself "the job of inventing the contemporary fictional Jew."
Although much of Bellow is "an obfuscatory whirlwind of
juvenile pep and philosophizing," he is one of the most
intelligent of contemporary novelists. Influenced by
Conrad, Dostoevsky, Kierkegaard and Sartre, Bellow is
impatient with the stereotype of the Jew, but in inventing
the contemporary fictional Jew, he transmorgifies him into
a giant or monster (as in The Adventures of Augie March),
or denies him the familiar incubus of anti-Semitism (Herzog).
In Seize the Day, Bellow best "comes to terms with his
characteristic themes and obsessions."

37   NATHAN, MONIQUE. "Saul Bellow." Esprit, 34 (September),
      363-70.
           An article, in French, on Saul Bellow's place among
      American novelists, and Herzog's place among American
      novels.

*38   POPESCU, PETRU. "Omul oscilant: Debutul lui Saul Bellow."
      Luceafărul (Bucharest), 9 (19 March), 1.
           Cited in Modern Language Association 1966 International
      Bibliography, p. 200.

39   RICHLER, MORDECAI. "Low Jinks." Spectator (25 March), p. 371.
           The Last Analysis is "self-parody Bellow; a minor lapse
      into self-indulgence." Only sporadically amusing, the play
      is filled "with theatrical tricks and vulgarities."

40   ROSENTHAL, T. G. "Trauma by Trauma." The Listener, 75
      (12 May), 697.
           The Last Analysis, which was a fiasco in New York, would
      not succeed in England: "...its terms of reference would
      go beyond the ken of the average theatregoer." The play is
      moving and very funny, although perhaps better enjoyed in
      the reading than on the stage.

41   RUBIN, LOUIS D. "Southerners and Jews." Southern Review, 2
      (Summer), 697-713.
           A disproportionate share of the best contemporary Amer-
      ican fiction has been written by Jewish writers who threaten
      the Southern hegemony in literature. Among these is Saul
      Bellow whose Herzog (pp. 705-708) is the novel of a man who
      "must discover the workable balance between society and the
      self, between the need to exist among other people and the
      compulsion to seek to define one's identity by them." This
      is characteristically a Jewish-American problem which Bellow
      elevates to a "symbol of man's unending discomfort with his
      human state."

1966

42   SAMUEL, MAURICE. "My Friend, The Late Moses Herzog." Mid-
       stream, 12 (April), 3-25.
           Samuel first compares Leopold Bloom and Herzog, seeing
       both heroes as representing two studies of Jewish assimila-
       tion. He then projects a living Herzog and writes a long
       narrative of their interactions. Herzog made a "mess of
       his life" because his Jewish feelings were too powerful for
       the small practical role he provided for them.

43   SHAW, PETER. "The Tough Guy Intellectual." Critical Quarterly,
       8 (Spring), 13-28.
           American writers characteristically develop heroes who
       are a combination of the lowbrow and the highbrow; the
       latest version is "the tough guy intellectual." This essay
       deals primarily with the heroes of Mailer and Bellow. Augie
       March is revealed as a tough guy intellectual in the book-
       stealing episodes; Henderson, a ludicrous tough guy, suc-
       ceeds in his spiritual quest because of his physical
       courage; Herzog is the tough guy when he returns to Chicago
       intending to kill Madeleine. In his prose style and in his
       public stance, Bellow himself adopts the role of the intel-
       lectual tough guy.

44   SHEED, WILFRID. Review of Under the Weather. Commonweal, 85
       (18 November), 199-201.
           Under the Weather is this year's lemon; novelists should
       not write for the stage. Bellow's "attempts at theatrical
       visualness are blundering and primitive." Some of the
       touches, however, "suggest that the real Mr. Bellow is not
       dead but sleeping."

45   SYMONS, JULIAN. "Bellow Before Herzog," in Critical Occasions.
       London: Hamish Hamilton, Ltd., pp. 112-118.
           A review of Henderson the Rain King, a "brilliantly
       comic, but finally rather unsatisfactory book." As an
       allegory, "it suffers from the double aim of writing about
       man's condition in the world and about moral problems
       specifically American."

46   UPHAUS, SUZANNE H. "From Innocence to Experience: A Study
       of Herzog." Dalhousie Review, 46 (Spring), 67-78.
           An attempt to trace the mental development of Herzog
       from a state of innocence to a state of experience--a de-
       velopment that gives rise to Herzog's final resolution to
       send no more letters. The development involves freeing
       himself from being determined--by others, by reality in-
       structors, by his female acquaintances, and by his own
       idiosyncracies. By freeing himself, he can at last affirm
       life.

47 WALCUTT, CHARLES C. Man's Changing Mask. Minneapolis: University of Minnesota Press, pp. 352-55.
Herzog is considered with other contemporary protagonists as an example of "the diminished self." Herzog himself hides behind a series of masks devised by Bellow;
while Herzog is well aware of his life situations, he hides
primarily behind the masks of comic and grotesque evasion.

48 WINEGARTEN, R. "Bellow's Suffering Joker." Jewish Observer
and Middle East Review, 15 (13 May), 17.
While the publication of The Last Analysis contributes
little to dramatic art, it is valuable as a key to Bellow's
own aims and intentions. Bellow here makes the most grave
concerns hilarious; he is able to laugh at life, which provides its own saving grace.

1967 A BOOKS

1 CLAYTON, JOHN J. "Saul Bellow: In Defense of Human Dignity."
Ph.D. dissertation, Indiana University, 316 pp. Listed in
Dissertation Abstracts, 27 (7: January), 2147A (Order
No. 66-14810).
Bellow's defense of man against cultural nihilism, and
the roots of that defense in Jewish and American cultural
tradition, are discussed as an introduction to a discussion
of each of the novels. Bellow's defense involves him in
three significant contradictions: he opposes cultural
nihilism but is himself a depressive; he rejects alienation,
but his characters are alienatees; he values individuality,
but discards it in his novels.

2 DETWEILER, ROBERT. Saul Bellow: A Critical Essay. Grand
Rapids, Mich.: Eerdmans, 48 pp.
An analysis of Bellow's literary art from a Christian
perspective. Bellow is "a type of the new Western man who
partakes of enough catholicity to project his singular
Jewish consciousness into the multifaceted 'Christian'
context." Detweiler justifies his approach by indicating
that "Christianity professes to encounter the whole man,
seeks the same kind of reconciliation that Bellow's art
embodies and encourages us not to theorize but to act."
A brief bibliography is included, pp. 47-48.

3 DOMMERGUES, PIERRE. Saul Bellow. Paris: Grasset, 250 pp.
In French: a selection of Bellow's essays representing
his key ideas, and selections of critical opinion on Bellow
and his heroes. The last chapter provides a "round table

1967

discussion" of Herzog by ten writers and critics (including
Mary McCarthy, Cyrille Arnavon and Helene Cixous), which is
interspersed with extracts from important critical articles.
Includes a bibliography of Bellow criticism in French.

*4   HUBER, GENEVIEVE. "The Uses of Anthropological Sources in
      Henderson the Rain King." M.A. thesis, University of
      Maryland.
          Cited in Cohen, 1974.A1.

5   MALIN, IRVING, ed. Saul Bellow and the Critics. New York:
      New York University Press, 227 pp.
          A collection of critical essays on Bellow, all previously
      published except for "Seven Images" by Malin (1967.B19).
      Contains "Saul Bellow" by Leslie Fiedler (1957.B9); "Saul
      Bellow: Novelist of Intellectuals" by Maxwell Geismar
      (1958.B5); "The Adventures of Saul Bellow: Progress of a
      Novelist" by Richard Chase (1959.B7); "Bellow's Dangling
      Men" by J. C. Levenson (1960.B7); "Saul Bellow: The Illu-
      sion of Environment" by Ralph Freedman (1960.B2); "Reality
      and the Hero: Lolita and Henderson the Rain King" by Daniel
      Hughes (1960.B5); "A Discipline of Nobility: Saul Bellow's
      Fiction" by Marcus Klein (1962.B4); "Caliban on Prospero:
      A Psychoanalytic Study of Seize the Day by Saul Bellow" by
      Daniel Weiss (1962.B14); "Bellow in Occupancy" by Earl
      Rovit (1965.B52); "Herzog: A Review" by Forrest Read
      (1964.B66); "The Complacency of Herzog" by John Aldridge
      (1966.B2); and a reprint of an essay by Bellow, "Where Do
      We Go from Here: The Future of Fiction."

6   MARKOS, DONALD W. "The Humanism of Saul Bellow." Ph.D. dis-
      sertation, University of Illinois. Listed in Dissertation
      Abstracts, 27 (11, May), 3875A (Order No. 67-6669).
          Considers Bellow the chief proponent today of the
      Emersonian self. His work has a transcendental element
      which focuses not on man's potential, but on his struggle
      to fulfill his potential. "In Bellow's fiction Emerson's
      self-reliant and Whitman's life-embracing man survives in
      a somewhat diminished and battle-scarred, but convincing
      form."

7   OPDAHL, KEITH M. The Novels of Saul Bellow: An Introduction.
      University Park, Pa.: Pennsylvania State University Press,
      200 pp. Bibliography, pp. 181-193.
          A revision of a dissertation, 1962.A1. Following an
      introductory chapter, Opdahl devotes one chapter to each of
      the novels through Herzog. Bellow is seen as continually
      returning to the opposition between the willful and the

loving, the skeptical and the believing. This conflict
pervades Bellow's style, the structure of his novels, and
the psychology of his protagonists; it is at once the unifying element of his fiction and the source of his difficulties. Opdahl explores the influence of this polarity on
Bellow's technique, explaining many of his shifts in form
and substance, and analyzing how it shapes theme and plot.
Emphasis is placed on the "religious" issues which drive
the heroes to rage, withdrawal and comic intensity.

8   ROVIT, EARL. Saul Bellow. University of Minnesota Pamphlets
    on American Writers. Minneapolis: University of Minnesota
    Press, 46 pp.
    .   Examines Bellow's work to show its most enduring qual-
    ities: a triumphant style and a predominant concern for
    defining what is viably human in modern life. Bellow's
    heroes share an uncomfortable belief in God, a strong sense
    of family (although usually estranged from their own), a
    feeling of being victimized by their own moral sense of
    right and wrong. The Bellow hero is imprisoned by himself;
    the despair this evokes is countered by Bellow's remarkable
    talent for comedy, so that he views the plight of modern
    man as pathetic rather than comic.

1967 B SHORTER WRITINGS

1   ALLEN, MICHAEL. "Idiomatic Language in Two Novels by Saul
    Bellow." Journal of American Studies, 1 (October), 275-80.
    Bellow's style, like Mark Twain's, "gives us the actual
    bodily set of a character." The Jewish idioms in The Adven-
    tures of Augie March "heighten, elaborate, and enrich."
    There is also a tension in the style: Augie's slickness of
    style and character is "continually arrested and transformed
    by an uneasily assertive moral weight inherent in the very
    rhythm...." Henderson's language, too, reflects his moral
    situation. He lacks an oral tradition which prevents some
    depth in his language, but, reflecting his tensed up phy-
    sique, his language does allow "strongly 'literary' phrases
    to be transformed and energized by the emphatic rhythms of
    a slang idiom...."

2   AXTHELM, PETER M. "The Full Perception: Bellow." The Modern
    Confessional Novel. New Haven, Conn.: Yale University
    Press, pp. 128-77.
    Herzog is viewed as a brilliantly realized confessional
    novel in which the hero moves beyond confession to begin a
    life of new meaning and richness. Axthelm traces stages in
    this confession, relates Herzog's confessional mode to

other modern confessional heroes, and examines how Herzog's
final perception paradoxically relates to both everything
and nothing.

3   BAKER, SHERIDAN. "Saul Bellow's Bout with Chivalry."
     Criticism, 9 (Spring), 109-122.
         More than any other modern novelist, Bellow is trying to
     work out an answer to "the dilemma of a faithless age that
     needs a faith." In attempting to find something noble and
     worthy for his heroes, Bellow turns to chivalric references.
     In Dangling Man he refers to the courtly lover and the
     knight, in The Victim the nighttime setting is something
     like an Arabian Night; Augie March pursues his own romantic
     quest, and the chivalric quest is at the center of Henderson
     the Rain King. Herzog is a "newly comic but seriously mad
     Quixote, laying the spirit of Romantic illusion."

4   BARUCH, FRANKLIN R. "Bellow and Milton: Professor Herzog in
     his Garden." Critique: Studies in Modern Fiction, 9
     (Summer), 74-83.
         Herzog's return to Ludeyville in the final scenes of the
     novel recalls Milton's creation of the setting for Adam and
     Eve's departure from the Garden of Eden. It is here that
     Herzog must come to terms with his failures, with the "un-
     changing quality of fallen nature's state." Bellow fills
     the scene with details of ritual and symbol, even while
     projecting the order and acceptance of life that had thus
     far eluded Herzog. The scene provides "an opening into the
     future, a world of new process and possibility."

5   BURGESS, ANTHONY. The Novel Now—A Student's Guide to Con-
     temporary Fiction. London: Faber and Faber, pp. 195-96,
     201.
         Very brief consideration of Bellow as a Jewish-American
     novelist.

6   CABAU, J. "Saul Bellow: Les Aventures d'Augie March," in
     La Prairie perdue. Paris: Le Seuil, pp. 313-329.
         In a book on the American novel (in French), one chapter
     is devoted to The Adventures of Augie March, with some
     attention given to Herzog.

7   CHAPMAN, ABRAHAM. "The Image of Man as Portrayed by Saul
     Bellow." College Language Association Journal, 10 (June),
     285-98.
         A common motif is explored in each of the novels: that
     man is on a quest, an intellectual journey "to fathom the
     meaning of his individual existence in a context of

grappling with the meaning of human existence." The men on such quests must see themselves as they are, without illusions and evasions, and with all of their human weaknesses.

8   CIXOUS, HÉLÈNE. "Situation de Saul Bellow." Lettres Nouvelles (March-April), pp. 130-45.
    In French, this essay focuses on Bellow's themes and vision, his support of the individual, and the significance of his comedy. Illustrations are drawn primarily from Herzog.

9   DOMMERGUES, PIERRE. "Recontre Avec Saul Bellow." Preuves, 191 (January), 38-47.
    An extensive interview with Bellow, in French, with wide-ranging questions on such topics as the place of the intellectual in American life, the American student movement, Bellow's attitude toward the romantic tradition, the involvement of writers in politics, the status of writers in society, a comparison of French and American writers, and Bellow's characterizations, particularly Herzog.

10   EDELMAN, L. "Editor's Notes." Jewish Heritage, 10 (Winter 1967/68), 3-4.
    A brief discussion of the relationship of Jewishness and Bellow's writings. "What Bellow affirms as Herzog's view of the human condition is the purest form of Jewish authenticity. His ability to propel it powerfully into the world's literary mainstream is his triumph and our gain."

11   FLEISCHMANN, WOLFGANG BERNARD. "The Contemporary 'Jewish Novel' in America." Jahrbuch für Amerikastudien, 12 (1967), 159-66.
    Herzog and several other contemporary "Jewish" novels are examined to establish that novels of such a genre are contending with "problems in contemporary American society representative in the ideas they present of states of mind more or less pervasive in that society, and endowed with novelistic structures which could accommodate the same plots under radically different ethnic or religious auspices."

12   FOSSUM, ROBERT H. "The Devil and Saul Bellow," in Mansions of the Spirit: Essays in Literature and Religion. New York: Hawthorn Books, pp. 345-57.
    Reprint of 1966.B19.

13   GUERARD, ALBERT J. "Saul Bellow and the Activists: On The Adventures of Augie March." Southern Review, 3 (July), 582-96.

1967

An attempt to place The Adventures of Augie March among
Bellow's first six novels and to place it in a particular
current of modern fiction. A Jewish imagination does not
define Bellow's literary position; rather it is his contri-
bution to "activist" novels--those works which espouse "a
belief in energy, vitality, sheer activity as moral goods."
The Adventures of Augie March has perhaps been the greatest
influence on writers holding an "activist" position.
Bellow has attempted to rescue the novel through an intensification of both language and adventure." The intensification of language is most apparent in his picaresque hero
who "must speak with the loose syntax of a man who does not
measure his words, with the authentic slang of the rebel
against middle-class decorum, and with the refinements of
philosophical allusion and poetic surprise."
This essay also serves as the introduction to the
Fawcett paperback edition of The Adventures of Augie March.
Translated into German and printed in 1974.B5.

14 HARPER, GORDON. "Saul Bellow: An Interview," in Writers at
Work, 3rd series. New York: Viking, pp. 175-96.
Reprint of 1966.B24.

15 HARPER, HOWARD M. "Saul Bellow--the Heart's Ultimate Need,"
in Desperate Faith: a Study of Bellow, Salinger, Mailer,
Baldwin, and Updike. Chapel Hill: University of North
Carolina Press, pp. 7-64.
A careful examination of Bellow's concern with "ultimate
questions" in each of the novels through Herzog. Bellow's
"honest, inspired, and relentless examination of the human
condition has given his work an interest which is both
timely and timeless."

16 HOGE, ALICE ALBRIGHT. "Saul Bellow Revisited, at Home and at
Work." Chicago Daily News Panorama Section, 41
(18 February), 5.
A record of an afternoon visit with Bellow in his apart-
ment near the University of Chicago. Bellow was working on
a novel "about the Second World War experience of Polish
Jews." He briefly discussed his childhood, and his dislike
of travel, celebrity status, and drama critics. Hoge also
recorded her impressions of a visit to Bellow's graduate
English literature class on "Character in the Modern Novel."

17 KRAMER, MAURICE. "The Secular Mode of Jewishness." Works,
1 (Autumn), 99-116.
Bellow's novels are considered in a section entitled
"Bear on a Roller Coaster" (pp. 110-16). In his novels

Bellow moves beyond the self-rejection of many Jewish heroes "by affirming the psychological truth of wishfulness." His heroes escape the negations of self-pity, although some suffering may be good if it keeps alive feeling. Bellow clearly insists on the human fates of his characters. He does not betray "the basic Jewish insistence that a man can be no more than a man."

18   MALIN, IRVING. Introduction to "Saul Bellow Sampler." Jewish Heritage, 10 (Winter 1967/68), 18-30.
        Comments on selections from Bellow's Seize the Day, Herzog, and The Victim which "move from alienation to community, hostility to peace. They do not sermonize, they speak urgently."

19   ____. "Seven Images," in Saul Bellow and the Critics. Edited by Irving Malin. New York: New York University Press, 142-76.
        Bellow communicates his concern for metaphysical questions through natural "images," which help make the reader experience the pains of existence. Malin discusses Bellow's use of the following images: weight, deformity, cannibalism, prison, beast, movement, and mirror.

*20   MANDEL, ARNOLD. Review of Herzog. Information juive (January).
        Cited in Dommergues, 1967.A3.

*21   MOHRT, MICHEL. Review of Herzog. Figaro littéraire (19 January).
        Cited in Dommergues, 1967.A3.

22   MORROW, PATRICK. "Threat and Accommodation: The Novels of Saul Bellow." Midwest Quarterly, 8 (Summer), 389-411.
        Bellow's heroes can be divided into two types—the admirable heroes (Augie, Henderson, and Herzog) who "develop means to accommodate their threats," and the unsympathetic heroes (Tommy, Asa, and Joseph) who escape their threats, but just barely. Tommy gains no self-knowledge at all; Asa merely assigns "simple truths as a defense against complex problems"; and Joseph, gaining self-awareness, at least fails meaningfully. Augie is self-determining and gains partial victories; the energetic Henderson ennobles himself through suffering; and Herzog accepts himself and thus gains some control over his life.

23   PETILLON, PIERRE-YVES. "Le Héros de Roman Américain a Pris de l'Age." Critique (Paris), 236 (January), 159-76.

1967

Herzog is seen as one of the most distinctive and mature
of modern American novels; it gives us an insight into the
human condition that has been achieved by few other
Americans.

24   RAIDER, RUTH. "Saul Bellow." Cambridge Quarterly, 2 (Spring),
      172-83.
           Ostensibly a review of Herzog and Tony Tanner's Saul
      Bellow, this essay comments on the first five novels and on
      Bellow's stature as a novelist. Raider finds Bellow to be
      a "minor comic novelist whose style is more often like mud
      than heavy pigment." Bellow's plots are insubstantial, his
      characters meagre, and his optimism unjustified.

*25   ROSENTHAL, JEAN. Review of Herzog. Réformé, 29 (April).
      Cited in Dommergues, 1967.A3.

26   RUBIN, LOUIS D. "The Experience of Difference: Southerners
      and Jews," in The Curious Death of the Novel. Baton Rouge:
      Louisiana State University Press, pp. 271-75.
      Reprint of 1966.B41.

27   STOCK, IRWIN. "The Novels of Saul Bellow." Southern Review,
      3 (Winter), 13-42.
           A book by book analysis of Bellow's novels through
      Herzog. In Bellow's work the bright affirmations of the
      Romantic Movement "are coming back to life." His work "is
      one passionate retaliation against all those forces in our
      culture that inhibit or pervert our power to feel...."
      Each of the novels is "an account of the adventures of a
      man of feeling."

28   TRACHTENBERG, STANLEY. "Saul Bellow's Luftmenschen: The
      Compromise with Reality." Critique: Studies in Modern
      Fiction, 9 (Summer), 37-61.
           Bellow's heroes, from Joseph to Herzog, have a self-
      qualified approach to reality. This stems from their
      luftmenschen qualities--with the desire to confront reality,
      "to operate in a fluid social environment," and from their
      desires to pursue the ideal. In "identifying the polarity
      between the real and the ideal that governs the movement,
      Bellow predicates both as alternative approaches to
      reality...." Trachtenberg traces this pattern in each of
      the first six novels, finding that Bellow, although unwill-
      ing to take the risks necessary to sound life at its great-
      est depth, nonetheless does brilliantly describe the
      conflicts that the search for reality creates.

29   TOWBRIDGE, CLINTON W.   "Water Imagery in Seize the Day."
     Critique: Studies in Modern Fiction, 9 (Summer), 62-73.
         By studying the water imagery in Seize the Day, we can
     come to understand the paradox of the novel, that life
     comes by drowning. The structure of Seize the Day is
     ironic; its theme is that man's real soul is born when his
     pretender soul is destroyed through suffering and pain.
     Bellow renders this theme primarily through the image of
     the drowning Wilhelm.

30   VAN EGMOND, PETER.   "Herzog's Quotation of Walt Whitman."
     Walt Whitman Review, 13 (June), 54-56.
         Upon his return to Ludeyville, Herzog, "talked to by
     tongues aromatic," finds himself virtually in the same
     setting that Whitman describes in "In Paths Untrodden."
     Herzog quotes from this poem in his letter to Dr. Zozo.
     The poem reflects the same searching for comrades, for
     physical and intellectual relationships as is found in
     Herzog's letters.

1968 A BOOKS

1   CLAYTON, JOHN J.   Saul Bellow: In Defense of Man. Blooming-
     ton: Indiana University Press, 273 pp. Selected bibliog-
     raphy, pp. 255-57.
         A revision of a dissertation, 1967.A1. Following an
     introduction in which he discusses Bellow's desperate
     affirmation and his cultural context, Clayton devotes part
     two to the "psychic pattern" of Bellow's fiction (including
     discussion of "alienation and masochism," "construction of
     self and the world," "the darkness," and "transformation.")
     Part three is devoted to individual studies of The Victim,
     Henderson the Rain King, and Herzog; part four concludes
     with a discussion of the unity and development of Bellow's
     fiction.
         Clayton sees Bellow as essentially a psychological novel-
     ist. He finds three interrelated contradictions in Bellow's
     work: while Bellow takes a stand against the cultural ni-
     hilism of the twentieth century, he is also a depressive
     whose imagination is horrified by the emptiness of modern
     life; while Bellow rejects the tradition of alienation and
     emphasizes brotherhood and community, most of his characters
     are masochists and alienated; and, finally, while Bellow
     seems to place a high value on individuality, in his novels
     he has been forced to discard individuality. Bellow's
     heroes approach an anonymous state of grace which is the
     opposite of the individuality Bellow loves and wishes to
     defend.

1968

2   CRAIG, HARRY E. "The Affirmation of the Heroes in the Novels
of Saul Bellow." Ph.D. dissertation, University of Pitts-
burgh, 137 pp. Listed in <u>Dissertation Abstracts</u>, 28
(12: June), 5012A (Order No. 68-7840).
    A thematic study of the positive affirmation--an affirma-
tion which bridges inner and outer worlds--in each of
Bellow's novels through <u>Herzog</u>.

3   HARTMAN, HUGH C. "Character, Theme and Tradition in The Novels
of Saul Bellow." Ph.D. dissertation, University of Washington, 332 pp. Listed in <u>Dissertation Abstracts</u>, 29
(3: September), 898A-899A (Order No. 68-12,691).
    Avoiding historical evaluations and ethnic comparisons,
this study analyzes the "artistry" of the novels in terms
of Bellow's imaginative reactions to the "distractions" of
life. The interrelationships between "flat" characters are
analyzed, as well as the disparities between claims and
actions of the protagonists. The central theme in the
novels is the modern individual's struggle to achieve a
single, complete identity.

1968 B SHORTER WRITINGS

1   AXTHELM, PETER. Review of <u>Mosby's Memoirs and Other Stories</u>.
<u>Newsweek</u>, 72 (28 October), 122, 125.
    Although this book of short stories falls short of
Bellow's best, "judged by any standards but those already
set by Bellow's own genius, these would be unequivocally
successful stories." The most brilliant, sensitive story
in the collection is "Looking for Mr. Green."

2   DONOGHUE, DENIS. "<u>Dangling Man</u>," in <u>The Ordinary Universe:
Soundings in Modern Literature</u>. New York: Macmillan,
pp. 194-203.
    All of Bellow's heroes through Herzog are viewed as
dangling men, as characters who are "more acutely aware
of the symptoms of their malaise than of its cause."
Reprinted in 1975.A4.

3   FISCH, HAROLD. "The Hero as Jew: Reflections on <u>Herzog</u>."
<u>Judaism</u>, 17 (1968), 42-54.
    Focuses on <u>Herzog</u> as a "particularization of Jewish
experience in mid-century," and an attempt to apply Jewish
solutions "to the problem of telling a coherent tale in an
increasingly incoherent world." <u>Herzog</u> has many parallels
to <u>Ulysses</u>, and may be viewed as "a kind of answer" to it.
Herzog survives, reaching out to a more wholesome, integrated existence, and while his survival does not

constitute salvation, it does indicate a fight against
alienation, emptiness, and despair.

4   FROHOCK, W. M. "Saul Bellow and His Penitent Picaro." South-
     west Review, 53 (Winter), 36-44.
        In surveying Bellow's novels, Frohock finds The Adven-
     tures of Augie March to be superior: "Augie talks, the
     others blurt." This novel is richer than other novels in
     the picaresque tradition because of a "presence of moral
     awareness." Unfortunately, Augie cannot enjoy the humor
     of his situation; with his knowledge, maturity and lack of
     innocence, he is more a penitent than a picaro.

5   HALL, JAMES. "Portrait of the Artist as a Self-Creating,
     Self-Vindicating, High Energy Man: Saul Bellow," in The
     Lunatic Giant in the Drawing Room: The British and American
     Novel since 1930. Bloomington: Indiana University Press,
     pp. 127-80.
        Hall considers Bellow's heroes as self-vindicating, self-
     creating men. They are problem-solvers, but become sur-
     prised and angered when their solutions don't work.

6   HOWE, IRVING. Introduction to Seize the Day in his edition of
     Classics of Modern Fiction. New York: Harcourt Brace and
     World, pp. 457-66.
        Discusses the setting, the character of Tommy Wilhelm,
     the minor characters, the style, and the use of poetry in
     Seize the Day.

7   KATZ, BILL. Review of Mosby's Memoirs and Other Stories.
     Library Journal, 93 (15 October), 3797.
        Brief notice: "It is significant that nothing is re-
     solved in any of the portraits, that Mr. Bellow is more
     fascinated with individual than with plot."

8   KAZIN, ALFRED. "Bellow's Purgatory." New York Review of
     Books, 10 (28 March), 32-36.
        Tracing Bellow's progress as a novelist from Dangling
     Man, Kazin focuses his discussion on Seize the Day, the
     most widely and genuinely admired of his works. Seize
     the Day most particularly reveals the pattern of constraint
     and expansions which can be seen in all of Bellow's novels.
     In contrast to the apparent expansive opulence of the city,
     Tommy is constrained, a nobody who ends up mourning himself.
     The use of the environment, Tommy's sensations in it, and
     his unrelenting self-examination, sustain our interest in
     the story and enable us to identify with him. Tommy's
     repeated confrontations with "knowing" characters in the

1968

story reflects Bellow's own distrust of "all the fashionable literary, critical, and psychological claims to
knowledge."
This essay also served as the "Introduction" to the
Fawcett paperback edition of Seize the Day.

9   LASSON, ROBERT. Review of Mosby's Memoirs and Other Stories.
     Book World (20 October), p. 6.
        A discussion between judge, prosecutor and defense on
     Bellow's collection of stories. The stories are found to
     be neither great nor significant. With no forward movement
     in them, they are not engaging.

10   LEWIN, LOIS S. "The Theme of Suffering in the Work of
     Bernard Malamud and Saul Bellow." Ph.D. dissertation,
     University of Pittsburgh. Listed in Dissertation Abstracts,
     28 (12: June), 5021A (Order No. 68-7846).
        The theme of suffering as a thematic center in Bellow's
     work is examined, with an attempt to understand how Bellow
     handles its psychological, social, and philosophical impli-
     cations. Chapter 1 deals with suffering in terms of its
     relationship to Jewish history and religion. Chapters 5 an
     and 6 examine how the suffering of Bellow's heroes arises
     from "their guilt, their failures, their inability to reach
     beyond their limited psyches to a comprehension of them-
     selves as a part of a larger world." For the Bellow hero,
     suffering is only transitional.

11   MUKHERJI, N. "The Bellow Hero." Indian Journal of English
     Studies, 9 (1968), 74-86.
        This is a brief survey of the first six novels which
     focuses upon the Bellow hero as a man of affirmation, one
     who believes in the dignity of man and the holiness of the
     heart's affections.

12   NOBLE, DAVID W. The Eternal Adam and the New World Garden.
     New York: George Braziller, pp. 216-23.
        Bellow's novels reveal a sense of the bankruptcy of the
     myth of the American Adam; the protagonists move toward new
     positions of spiritual commitment and moral responsibility.

13   OVERBECK, PAT T. "The Women in Augie March." Texas Studies
     in Literature and Language, 10 (Fall), 471-84. The women
     appearing in The Adventures of Augie March provide struc-
     tural support for the novel; Augie's straight paths inevi-
     tably wind around a woman in circles of love and attraction.
     This pattern is exemplified in his relationship with
     Rebecca March, Mama, Grandma Lausch, Esther and Thea
     Fenchel, Mimi Villars, Stella Chesney, and others.

1968

14   PHILLIPS, LOUIS. "The Novelist as Playwright: Baldwin,
      McCullers, and Bellow, in Modern American Drama: Essays in
      Criticism. Edited by William E. Taylor. Deland, Fla.:
      Everett Edwards, pp. 145-62.
         Bellow, like Baldwin and McCullers, has felt the need to
      use a dramatic form to express and develop themes that have
      formed the basis of his novels. Bellow's efforts have
      failed; in The Last Analysis, the mental comedy, Bellow's
      forté, is missing for it is incapable of being expressed
      on stage through physical actions.

15   PINSKER, SANFORD S. "The Schlemiel as Metaphor: Studies in
      the Yiddish and American Jewish Novel." Ph.D. dissertation,
      University of Washington, 278 pp. Listed in Dissertation
      Abstracts, 28 (9: March), 3679A-80A (Order No. 68-3873).
         The schlemiel, a character plagued by bad luck which is
      usually the result of his own ineptness, emerged as a key
      figure in the Yiddish literature of East European ghettos
      in the mid-nineteenth century. Five authors are considered
      here (Mendele, Aleicheim, Singer, Malamud, and Bellow); for
      Bellow, "the schlemiel tends to have more psychologically
      oriented problems than either the schlemiels of traditional
      Yiddish literature or the socio-economic bunglers of Sholom
      Aleichem." The contemporary schlemiel sees his problem,
      but no solution.
         Revised and published: 1971.B25.

16   RABAN, J. "Narrative: Dramatized Consciousness," in Tech-
      nique in Modern Fiction. London: Edward Arnold, 49-55.
         A passage from Herzog (when Herzog is on the train,
      en route to Martha's Vineyard) is analyzed in terms of its
      dramatized consciousness. Bellow is seen as blending both
      vernacular and stream of consciousness traditions; the re-
      sult is an amazingly complex mixture in which there is no
      consistency of time, logic, or language. All this reflects
      Bellow's vision of the life of an intellectual in America
      as "one of massive personal disintegration."

17   SAMUELS, CHARLES T. "Action and Idea in Saul Bellow." The
      Atlantic, 222 (November), 126-30.
         In a review of Mosby's Memoirs and Other Stories,
      Samuels discusses Bellow's major problem as a writer: the
      inability to fuse action and idea. He succeeds best in
      Seize the Day and in the short story "Looking for Mr. Green,"
      but most of the short stories in this collection "seem
      undernourished versions of his longer works." The short
      story form is not good for Bellow: it "simply does not
      provide him with room sufficient for the flexing of mental
      muscles."

1968

*18 SCHEER-SCHÄZLER, BRIGITTE. A Taste for Metaphors: Die
     Bildersprache als Interpretationsgrundlage des modernen
     Romans, dargestellt an Saul Bellows Herzog. Modern
     Sprachen, Schriftenreihe 2. Wien: Verband der
     Osterreichischen Neuphilologen.
     Cited in Modern Language Association International
     Bibliography, 1 (1970), 122.

19   SCOTT, NATHAN A., JR. "Sola Gratia: The Principle of Bellow's
     Fiction," in his edition of Adversity and Grace: Studies
     in Recent American Literature. Chicago: University of
     Chicago Press, pp. 27-57.
         Bellow writes from a tradition of fiction "whose prin-
     cipal area of inquiry is the phenomenology of selfhood."
     His characters while being "theoreticians"--pursuing their
     inquiry into the meaning of human existence--are yet very
     animated and exuberant. What pervades Bellow's fiction,
     though, is a profoundly religious rendering of experience,
     with dramas of reconciliation, redemption, and
     justification.
         Reprinted: 1968.B20; revised and reprinted: 1973.B29.

20   _____. Craters of the Spirit. Washington, D.C.: Corpus
     Publications, pp. 233-65.
         Reprint of 1968.B19.

21   SHULMAN, ROBERT. "The Style of Bellow's Comedy." Publications
     of the Modern Language Association of America, 83 (March),
     109-17.
         Bellow's ideological comedy relates him more closely to
     intellectual humorists such as Rabelais, Burton, Sterne,
     Melville, and Joyce rather than to writers in the picaresque
     tradition. Bellow's comedy illuminates and celebrates the
     present, particularly in his open-form books--The Adventures
     of Augie March and Herzog--which in this essay are discussed
     in detail. Bellow's comedy, expressed in style, situation,
     and character, also helps to unify these somewhat formless
     books.

22   TAJUDDIN, MOHAMMAD. "The Tragicomic Novel: Camus, Malamud,
     Hawkes, Bellow." Ph.D. dissertation, Indiana University,
     188 pp. Listed in Dissertation Abstracts, 28 (7: January),
     2698A-99A (Order No. 67-15,168).
         "Tragicomic" refers to fiction which is primarily tragic,
     but which is set in a wider context of the non-tragic and
     comic. These four novelists write in this mode, and their
     affinities can be seen in (1) their attitude toward empirical
     reality; (2) the values of compromise and practicality; and
     (3) the use of humor and irony.

WRITINGS ABOUT SAUL BELLOW, 1944-1976

23   TELLER, JUDD L. "From Yiddish to Neo-Brahmin," in <u>Strangers
     and Natives--The Evolution of the American Jew from 1921 to
     the Present</u>. New York: Delacorte Press, pp. 251-72.
     Discusses the influence of the Yiddish literary tradition
     on Bellow and other contemporary American writers.

24   VOGEL, DAN. "Saul Bellow's Vision Beyond Absurdity: Jewish-
     ness in Herzog." <u>Tradition: A Journal of Orthodox Jewish
     Thought</u>, 9 (Spring), 65-79.
     Jewish fiction has come to reflect the emotions and con-
     cerns of the non-Jewish public, largely because there is an
     important past to which the Jew is related. The sense of
     permanence in a world of flux enables a writer like Bellow
     to offer a "vision beyond absurdity." In <u>Herzog</u> there is
     a sense of the past, but also concern for the immediate
     present and for the future. "The most important implica-
     tion of Herzog's spiritual journey is Bellow's declaration
     through his protagonist that God is truly alive; but more
     that He cares; and still more that He pays individual
     attention."

25   WEBER, RONALD. "Bellow's Thinkers." <u>Western Humanities
     Review</u>, 22 (Autumn), 305-13.
     In all of Bellow's fiction, "the intellect ranges freely
     and finds open expression in the language of thought; but
     in this fiction men can also be victimized and destroyed
     through the activity of the mind." Herzog, in particular,
     has a compulsion to embrace everything in his head, and
     this compulsion almost ruins him. Bummidge, in <u>The Last
     Analysis</u>, is also struggling to survive in an environment
     of ideas, and for him the explained life is as unbearable
     as the unexplained life.

1969 A BOOKS

1   ALLEN, MARY L. "The Flower and the Chalk: The Comic Sense of
     Saul Bellow." Ph.D. dissertation, Stanford University,
     303 pp. Listed in <u>Dissertation Abstracts</u>, 29 (11: May),
     3997A (Order No. 69-8141).
     A topical discussion of Bellow's comedy focusing upon
     Bellow's comic affirmative vision, his comedy of situation,
     comedy of character, and comedy of language. One chapter
     is devoted to a discussion of <u>Herzog</u> as a paradigm of the
     arguments relating to the tragic and comic visions.

2   MALIN, IRVING. <u>Saul Bellow's Fiction</u>. Crosscurrents/Modern
     Critiques Series. Carbondale, Ill.: Southern Illinois
     University Press.

1969

First Malin establishes Bellow's "world," using as a
basis his first published story, "Two Morning Monologues."
He then discusses five recurrent themes (moha, madness,
time, masquerade, and Jewishness), devotes a chapter to a
discussion of characters, and then two chapters to the
"images and styles which express or incarnate themes and
character." The final chapter is devoted to Herzog, which
Malin sees as a culmination of Bellow's characteristic
themes, images, and styles.

3   MAUROCORDATO, ALEXANDRE. Les quatre dimensions du Herzog de
    Saul Bellow. 6 (Archiv des Lettres Modernes, No. 102;
    Archives Anglo-americaines, No. 14). Paris: Lettres
    Modernes, 94 pp.
        An extensive study, in French, of four aspects of Herzog:
    "La première correspond à l'espace où se situe l'action et
    dont les coordonnées sont, d'une part, la disposition de
    l'ouvrage, les inervalles et les pauses qui le découpent
    dans sa longueur, de l'autre sa géographie intérieure, les
    lieux ou l'auteur nous entraîne les couches alluvionaires
    qu'il explore. La seconde correspond au temps qu'emprisonne
    tout roman et que déroule sous nos yeux son horlogerie
    secrète, avec ses effects d'accéleration et de
    ralentissement. ...La troisième dimension d'une oeuvre
    romanesque en formule la durée, c'est-à-dire, le rapport
    variable entre l'espace et le temps qu'elle contient.
    ...la quatrième dimension...touche au mystère des rapports
    entre le créateur et son oeuvre." A brief bibliography is
    included.

4   NOREEN, ROBERT G. "Bearing Witness to Life: The Novels of
    Saul Bellow." Ph.D. dissertation, The University of
    Chicago.
        While Bellow acknowledges that a man's life often seems
    paradoxical--his heroes have the strong desire to be "truly
    human," but the choices and alternatives open to them force
    them into positions which deny their humanity--he also sug-
    gests in his novels a way to live with this paradox. This
    study traces a common theme in the novels, the theme that
    a man can best realize his potential as a human being
    through a struggle to synthesize his disparate experiences,
    through a struggle to overcome the forces which pull him in
    opposite directions. Each of Bellow's heroes strives to
    find the still point, the axial lines, the equilibrium, or
    the balance between absolute freedom and stifling determina-
    tion, between the responsibility he owes himself and the
    responsibility he owes others, between selfishness and self-
    lessness, between giving and receiving, between a life

governed by one's ideas and a life governed by one's feel-
ings. Striking the balance between these extremes would
enable the hero to achieve a life which is truly human,
truly most free from restrictive bonds. This study also
shows how Bellow has expressed faith in man's ability to
assert and to establish those values which would make his
life more meaningful. In expressing such faith in his
novels, Bellow justifies man's existence and bears witness
to his life.

1969 B SHORTER WRITINGS

1   ALTER, ROBERT. "Saul Bellow: A Dissent from Modernism," in
    After the Tradition. New York: E. P. Dutton, pp. 95-115.
    Revision of 1964.B1.

2   ANON. Review of Mosby's Memoirs and Other Stories. Choice,
    6 (September), 810.
        Brief review: The stories are not so brilliant as
    Bellow's novels. "The people are too justly ticked off,
    the constructions are too involved, the titles are too
    witty, the author's hand too evident." The stories, un-
    fortunately, do not add too much to our understanding of
    Bellow's work.

3   ANON. Review of Mr. Sammler's Planet. Antioch Review, 29
    (Winter, 1969/1970), 587.
        In this, Bellow's best novel, Sammler is "a symbolic
    declaration for rationality, inner order, imitation of
    higher rather than lower representations." Ignorance, here
    or on the moon, is the ultimate evil; we must always return
    to the knowledge already in our hearts.

4   ATKINS, ANSELM. "The Moderate Optimism of Saul Bellow's
    Herzog." The Personalist, 50 (Winter), 117-29.
        Explores the dialectic by which Herzog's moderate opti-
    mism emerges from the extremes of innocence and experience.
    Herzog contrasts his innocent attitude to the world with
    two forms of realism--the brutal realism of the Himmelstein
    types and the pessimistic, intellectual realism of the
    Shapiros. Herzog goes beyond innocence and experience, with
    each modifying the other, to a highly refined "chastened
    optimism."

5   BEZANKER, ABRAHAM. "The Odyssey of Saul Bellow." Yale Review,
    58 (Spring), 359-71.
        No other writer today has Bellow's "speculative bril-
    liance or his remarkable talent for assimilating the

1969

literary and intellectual traditions of the West and for
re-shaping them into rich, vivid and persuasive characterizations." All of his characters wear their hearts on
their sleeves; they have a reluctant gregariousness, but
they do affirm man as a social animal. While each hero is
something of a fool, and they do find love fragile and
ephemeral, they all, through their actions and words,
believe that the spiritual informs the physical.

6   BOULGAR, JAMES D.   "Puritan Allegory in Four Modern Novels."
      Thought, 44 (1969), 413-32.
           In Herzog (as in Cozzens' By Love Possessed, Ellison's
      Invisible Man, and O'Conner's The Last Hurrah), the alle-
      gorical religious pattern raises the significance of the
      novel above the ordinary. Puritan allegorical patterns of
      Election and Trials of Vocation can be seen in Herzog.

7   CAMPBELL, JEFF H.   "Bellow's Intimations of Immortality:
      Henderson the Rain King." Studies in the Novel, 1 (Fall),
      323-33.
           Henderson the Rain King is enriched by numerous literary
      allusions, particularly the implicit parodies of motifs
      typical of Dreiser, Faulkner, Hemingway, Camus, and Golding.
      These parodies, early in the book, imply the rejection of
      contemporary clichés as answers to Henderson's quest, and
      pave the way for a more central and serious allusion to
      Wordsworth's "Intimations" ode. A comparison of the steps
      in Henderson's quixotic quest with the stages of growth
      described in Wordsworth's ode suggest a meaningful metaphor
      to explain the book's central affirmation.

*8   CIANCIO, RALPH.   "The Achievement of Saul Bellow's Seize the
      Day," in Literature and Theology. Edited by Thomas F.
      Staley and Lester F. Zimmerman. University of Tulsa
      Department of English Monograph Series, Tulsa, Okla.:
      University of Tulsa Press, pp. 49-80.
           Cited in Adelman and Divorkin, p. 56: 1972.B1.

9   CURLEY, DOROTHY NYREN, and MAURICE KRAMER.   "Saul Bellow," in
      A Library of Literary Criticism, Vol. 1. New York:
      Frederick Ungar, pp. 85-94.
           Twenty-six selected excerpts from published criticism,
      each about a paragraph in length, representing the predom-
      inant critical views of Bellow's works. The excerpts focus
      both on Bellow's writings generally and on specific novels.

10   DALTON, ELIZABETH.   Review of Mosby's Memoirs and Other
      Stories. Commentary, 47 (April), 69-70.

Taken together, the stories in this collection do not
have much impact. They are conceptions, rather than experiences. They lack the emotional density that should shape
and fill out the idea behind a story.

*11 DAVIS, WILLIAM V. "Bellow's Herzog." Orion, 118 (1969), 73.
     Cited in Modern Language Association International
     Bibliography, 1 (1970), 122.

12   DEMAREST, DAVID P., JR. "The Theme of Discontinuity in Saul
     Bellow's Fiction: 'Looking for Mr. Green' and 'A Father-
     to-Be.'" Studies in Short Fiction, 6 (1969), 175-86.
     These two short stories provide an excellent introduc-
     tion to Bellow's general vision. Both ask which of two
     responses to life is appropriate--a search for intellectual
     order or a willingness to take life as it is. Each suggests
     that both attitudes are inevitable and appropriate. The
     heroes of these stories prefigure the more fully self-aware
     character of Herzog.

13   FIEDLER, LESLIE. "Saul Bellow," in On Contemporary Literature.
     Edited by R. Kostelanetz. New York: Avon, pp. 286-95.
     Reprint of 1957.B9.

14   FLAMM, DUDLEY. "Herzog--Victim and Hero." Zeitschrift für
     Anglistik und Amerikanistik, 17 (No. 2), 174-88.
     Traditionally, the victim is seen in literature as the
     scapegoat or sacrificial object, and the hero is seen as a
     figure of some standing who has a chance to succeed. In
     Herzog, "an interesting fusion of these roles takes place,
     suggesting a resultant--victim as hero." Since Herzog com-
     bines these roles, the novel "proposes itself as the vehi-
     cle for the thematic synthesis of ideas in his earlier
     fiction," in which Bellow presented both victims and heroes.

15   GIBSON, WALKER. Persona: A Style Study for Readers and
     Writers. New York: Random House, pp. 31-40.
     Examines the "bravura" performance of mixed styles in
     Herzog.

16   HOFFMAN, MICHAEL J. "From Cohn to Herzog." Yale Review, 58
     (Spring), 342-58.
     Hemingway's Robert Cohn, the archetypal Jew in modern
     American fiction, has now assumed the center of the literary
     stage in Herzog. Cohn and Herzog have many similarities:
     Herzog is still "the bungling, apologetic, relationship-
     conscious, articulate-at-the-wrong-times Jew." The wide-
     spread interest in Herzog possibly signals a fundamental

1969

change in American culture. Hemingway attempted to produce
a serious heroic vision; Bellow, in recognizing the absurdity of human life, has a vision which is never totally without humor. Herzog's extremes of emotion and intellect
belong to the secularized American community today, not
just the Jews.

17   KNIPP, THOMAS R. "The Cost of Henderson's Quest." Ball State
University Forum, 10 (Spring), 37-39.
    Most critics have ignored the plot of Henderson the Rain
King, but a careful study of what "Henderson does and his
reasons for doing so will deepen one's awareness...of the
high cost of resurrection and the dangerous consequences of
self-fulfillment in the modern world."

18   LUCKO, PETER. "Herzog—Modell der acceptance: Eine
Erwiderung." Zeitschrift für Anglistik und Amerikanistik,
17 (1969), 189-95.
    An analysis, in German, of the characterization and
themes in Herzog.

19   NADON, ROBERT J. "Urban Values in Recent American Fiction:
A Study of the City in the Fiction of Saul Bellow, John
Updike, Philip Roth, Bernard Malamud, and Norman Mailer."
Ph.D. dissertation, University of Minnesota, 450 pp.
Listed in Dissertation Abstracts International, 30
(6: December), 2543A (Order No. 69-20,041).
    Of these writers, only Bellow and Mailer are truly city
writers. The city constantly threatens the Bellow hero:
"His early heroes fear the city and seek to escape it; his
later heroes learn to accommodate and often enjoy the city."
His characters also seek community within the city.

20   NORMAND, J. "L'homme mystifié: Les héros de Bellow, Albee,
Styron, et Mailer." Etudes Anglaises, 22 (1969), 370-85.
    Among Bellow heroes, this essay focuses upon Herzog, who
is regarded as "une somme de discordances, une mosaique
humaine." Herzog represents a synthesis of the extreme
character types created by Bellow. In French.

21   PINSKER, SANFORD. Review of Mosby's Memoirs and Other Stories.
Judaism, 18 (Summer), 377-82.
    Bellow's Mosby's Memoirs is Bellow's "stopgap measure,
a way of keeping his name before the public" while working
on another novel. The stories do reveal an increased range
of situations for Bellow, but whining is still the "most
persistent response" of his claustrophobic characters.

22   PORTER, MARVIN GILBERT. "Herzog: A Transcendental Solution
      to an Existential Problem." Forum (Houston), 7 (Spring),
      32-36.
         This study of the novel traces Herzog's painful efforts
      to formulate a "synthesis" to shore up his disintegrating
      life. "He solves his problem, finally, by moving through
      existentialism to transcendentalism."
         This essay appears in slightly different form in
      Porter, 1974.A3.

23   RAHV, PHILIP. "Saul Bellow's Progress," in Literature and the
      Sixth Sense. Boston: Houghton Mifflin, pp. 392-97.
         Reprint of 1964.B65.

24   RICHARDSON, JACK. "Chasing Reality." New York Review of
      Books, 12, No. 5 (13 March), 12-14.
         A review of Mosby's Memoirs and Other Stories. After
      surveying Bellow's novels--those works which provide the
      "antic perversity of life, its refusal to live up to the
      simplest or most elaborate human expectation"--Richardson
      comments on two of the stories in this collection, "Mosby's
      Memoirs" and "Leaving the Yellow House," both of which also
      convey a feeling of mortality, "a slow illumination of the
      final trick that life plays on the human spirit."

25   ROSENTHAL, MELVYN. "The American Writer and His Society: The
      Response to Estrangement in the Works of Nathaniel Hawthorne,
      Randolph Bourne, Edmund Wilson, Norman Mailer, Saul Bellow."
      Ph.D. dissertation, University of Connecticut, 185 pp.
      Listed in Dissertation Abstracts, 29 (9: March), 3108A
      (Order No. 69-2175).
         This study explores the various tensions generated in
      the works of these writers from the failure of America to
      realize its own ideal. Bellow, in contrast to Mailer,
      "insists that we cannot withdraw from our social identity,
      for to do so would be to repudiate our life-giving bond
      with the human community." Bellow instead insists that
      "we must find an ambiguous but exuberant joy in our human-
      ity, a joy that is more precious precisely because of the
      threat of alienation and despair."

26   SCHULZ, MAX F. "Saul Bellow and the Burden of Selfhood," in
      Radical Sophistication: Studies in Contemporary Jewish-
      American Novelists. Athens, Ohio: Ohio University Press,
      pp. 110-153.
         Explores the burden of selfhood in Bellow's works in
      relation to the thematic tension between the head and the
      heart, the group and the individual, and character and

1969

narrative. Special emphasis is placed on Blake's influence on Bellow.

27 SHERMAN, BERNARD. The Invention of the Jew--Jewish-American Education Novels (1916-1964). New York: Thomas Yoseloff, pp. 132-45.
 The Adventures of Augie March is considered as a Jewish education novel, a bildungsroman in a Jewish context.

1970 A BOOKS

1 COHEN, SARAH B. "The Comic Elements in the Novels of Saul Bellow." Ph.D. dissertation, Northwestern University, 280 pp. Listed in Dissertation Abstracts International, 30 (7: January), 3000A-01A (Order No. 70-28).
 A systematic and extended analysis of the comic elements in Bellow's novels, including focus upon the comedy of character, comedy of situation, comedy of ideas, and the comedy of language.
 Revised and published: 1974.A1.

2 MICHAEL, BESSIE. "What's the Best Way to Live? A Study of the Novels of Saul Bellow." Ph.D. dissertation, Lehigh University, 230 pp. Listed in Dissertation Abstracts International, 30 (12: June), 5451A-52A (Order No. 70-10,612).
 Each of Bellow's characters answers this question in different ways because each has a particular set of givens; but they all share in struggling and suffering, they are all "fortified" with aspirations, hope, and the persistent love of life.

3 PORTER, MARVIN GILBERT. "The Novels of Saul Bellow: A Formalist Reading." Ph.D. dissertation, University of Oregon, 239 pp. Listed in Dissertation Abstracts International, 31 (3: September), 1287A (Order No. 15,352).
 A formalist analysis of Bellow's novels which attempts to reveal the organic relation between structure and texture in the novels, and to gain appreciation for the finely tuned quality of Bellow's humanity and special vision. John Crowe Ransom's "structure-texture" theory is used to demonstrate how theme is embodied in form.
 Revised and published: 1974.A3.

4 RODRIGUES, EUSEBIO L. "Quest for the Human: Theme and Structure in the Novels of Saul Bellow." Ph.D. dissertation, University of Pennsylvania, 292 pp. Listed in Dissertation Abstracts International, 31 (6: December), 2936A-37A (Order No. 70-25,722).

Bellow's novels are dramatizations of a single dominant
theme: the quest for the human and humaneness. Each of
the novels is examined as a fictional structure which
Bellow has built to house his theme. One chapter focuses
upon Bellow's language.

5   WIETING, MOLLY S. "A Quest for Order: The Novels of Saul
        Bellow." Ph.D. dissertation, University of Texas, Austin,
        234 pp. Listed in Dissertation Abstracts International, 30
        (7: January), 3030A-31A (Order No. 69-21,905).
            As they seek order in their lives, Bellow's protagonists
        reflect Jewish attitudes and Jewish cultural values, par-
        ticularly as they move "from alienation to reconciliation
        with the community and as they use family relationships to
        symbolize that movement." Three distinct stages of develop-
        ment in this transition are traced for each of the heroes.

1970 B SHORTER WRITINGS

1   ANON. "In Search of Order." Times Literary Supplement
        (9 July), p. 749.
            A review of Mr. Sammler's Planet. Sammler "is a model
        of old-fashioned rectitude," one who values the past. In
        contrast to the philosophy of many of the younger genera-
        tion, Bellow's novel preaches "the values of a purified
        tradition, the necessity of rules, the weakness of the un-
        aided self." These are stern words for a generation who
        "resent all external imperatives." At his best, Bellow is
        a "mixture of Forster and Camus."

2   ANON. Review of Mr. Sammler's Planet. American Libraries, 1
        (July), 714.
            Brief notice of the novel as a "Notable Book" of 1970.
        Sammler is Bellow's best character yet.

3   ANON. Review of Mr. Sammler's Planet. Booklist, 66 (1 April),
        953.
            A brief review: in the novel, "the counterpoint of per-
        sonalities, subplots, and incidents constitutes a tragi-
        comic commentary on twentieth century urban life, but it
        is Sammler's considered reflections on that life that
        dominate...." The novel "asks basic questions about how
        we live and what we live for at this chaotic point in
        history."

4   ANON. Review of Mr. Sammler's Planet. Choice, 7 (May),
        382-83.
            A brief review: This is a major work with the theme of
        "the diminished possibility of a private life in a society

1970

no longer bourgeois." The style, not as accomplished as in
Bellow's earlier works, is somewhat "too relaxed for full
enjoyment."

5 ANON. Review of Mr. Sammler's Planet. Publishers Weekly, 198
   (14 December), 40.
      Brief notice of the paperback edition of Mr. Sammler's
   Planet. It is a "warm and human, funny and sad, and spec-
   ulative novel on several levels."

6 ANON. Review of Mr. Sammler's Planet. Virginia Quarterly
   Review, 46 (Spring), xl-xli.
      This is a first rate novel, but some scenes are "aston-
   ishingly dull" and the book is too "rigidly devoted to one
   racial group and its problems."

7 ANON. "Saul Bellow: Seer with a Civil Heart." Time, 95
   (9 February), 81-84.
      It is time to admit that Bellow is a "seer." With his
   new novel, Bellow clears "a place in the rubble where man
   can stand." Sammler is a "kind of reference volume in
   which fools and others can look to find what sanity is."
   Because Sammler comes to terms with his life, this is
   Bellow's most exciting, brilliant book: "...it deals with
   those perceptions beyond intellectual argument through
   which men come to know the world for what it is and themselves for what it makes of them." (The review is accompa-
   nied by a biographical sketch, See 1970.B20).

8 ATCHITY, JOHN KENNETH. "Bellow's Mr. Sammler: The Last Man
   Given for Epitome." Research Studies, 38 (March), 46-54.
      Novels like Mr. Sammler's Planet do not readily lend
   themselves to the usual critical categories, for they are
   almost without plot. This novel's inspiration is an idea
   rather than a story, and the idea is conveyed through characterization. Sammler must find the essence of reality in
   everyday, routine concerns and events, however petty. Too
   designed a pattern of action would not convince the reader
   that art, and particularly the novel, has a meaningful function in his life.

9 BAIM, JOSEPH, and DAVID P. DEMAREST, JR. "Henderson the Rain
   King: A Major Theme and a Technical Problem," in A Modern
   Miscellany. Edited by David Demarest, Jr., Lois A. Lamdin,
   and Joseph Baim. Carnegie Series in English, 11 (1970),
   53-63.
      Baim deals with the major theme; Demarest with the tech-
   nical problem. Bellow's approach to the problem of identity

in the novels is mystical or intuitive, not ethnic. The
discovery of identity begins through an effort to escape
intellection. For Henderson, truth comes in "blows," not
by deliberate searching. As he "experiences" death, his
striving to establish identity ceases. A technical problem
in the novel is that Bellow attempts to make Henderson both
a rounded character and a two-dimensional comic fall guy.
In doing so he fails to achieve a satisfactory synthesis of
reality and fantasy. Consequently, our attitudes toward
Henderson are not consistent.

10   BAIM, JOSEPH. "Escape from Intellection: Saul Bellow's
        Dangling Man." University Review, 37 (Autumn), 28-34.
           Bellow's approach to the problem of identity is not in
        the Jewish humanist tradition, but rather in the mystical
        tradition. Bellow's heroes seek illumination rather than
        pragmatic solutions to their problems. Joseph in Dangling
        Man provides one of the clearer examples: he comes to
        recognize that reason is self-defeating, and logic is
        limited; illumination and insight may come spontaneously
        when "the whole of one's capacity to respond intuitively
        is totally engaged and intellectual responses are
        impossible."

11   BAYLEY, JOHN. "More Familiar than Novel." The Listener, 84
        (9 July), 51.
           Mr. Sammler's Planet draws forth our assent, but does
        not move us. The reader has known it all before. There is
        a kind of "defeatism" in Bellow's skills.

12   BRAINE, JOHN. "Bellow's Planet." National Review, 22
        (10 March), 264.
           Braine berates Bellow for being a member of the American
        literary establishment "Family," and for writing
        Mr. Sammler's Planet under the influences of "Family"
        orthodoxy.

13   BRENDON, PIERS. "Tottering Civilisation." Books and Bookmen,
        15 (September), 42.
           In Mr. Sammler's Planet Bellow is sensitive to the
        obscene negation of humane values which threaten to col-
        lapse western civilization. The novel is a haunting one,
        with the moon silently riding through the skies, "a symbol
        not only of chastity, but of madness and death."

14   BROYARD, ANATOLE. Review of Mr. Sammler's Planet. New York
        Times Book Review (1 February), pp. 1, 40.

1970

> Sammler seems timeless, classical, disinterested. He is one of Bellow's best creations—embodying Bellow's ideas and yet remaining convincing in his own right. Sammler has the perspectives of age; his only need is to understand.

15 BRYANT, JERRY H. The Open Decision—The Contemporary American Novel and Its Intellectual Background. New York: Free Press, pp. 341-69.

A discussion of Bellow's major themes and the "salient pattern" in the novels. The main character in each of the novels attempts to free himself from the limits of his condition in order to achieve a "superior" life or a "grand synthesis," while being confronted with the impossibility of that achievement.

16 COOK, BRUCE. "Mr. Sammler's Planet is Basically Comic, But Weighty with Wisdom." National Observer, 9 (26 January), 25.

The novel is disappointing, having not much plot and less story; it exists primarily as a vehicle "to transport the ruminations and opinions" of Sammler. Sammler never moves nor changes, and thus the novel has little life. Since the other characters are essentially stock types, life comes in only with Bellow's wisdom and eloquence.

17 CORDESSE, GÉRARD. "L'unité de Herzog." Caliban, 7 (1970), 99-113.

In French, this essay seeks to discover the unifying factors in Herzog, a novel which is both a psychological study and a philosophical debate.

18 DeMOTT, BENJAMIN. "Saul Bellow and the Dogmas of Possibility." Saturday Review, 53 (7 February), 25-28, 37.

The spirited comedy and "intermittent analytical brilliance" are praiseworthy in Mr. Sammler's Planet, but at bottom the novel suffers from "a defect of sympathy." Sammler's vision and sympathy are limited, but also invulnerable. This could provide a situation for satire, but the novel "undertakes to pass itself off as a genuine imaginative encounter with, and penetration of, forces and beings it despises." Sammler doesn't confront dramatically the issues that really matter today. The sage is overprotected.

19 DITSKY, JOHN. "The Watch and Chain of Henry James." University of Windsor Review, 6 (Fall), 91-101.

In this review article of The French Lieutenant's Woman and Mr. Sammler's Planet, Ditsky finds Bellow's novel one

of depth and resonance, endowed with an untimely sense of
time, in which plot doesn't matter, and the characters are
better than the types they really are. It is a novel in
the Jamesian manner, "dealing with issues in our time," but
having been deliberately set against another time.

20   DUFFY, MARTHA. "Some People Come Back Like Hecuba." Time,
     95 (9 February), 82.
         An interview/profile upon the publication of Mr. Sammler's
     Planet, with a brief discussion of Bellow's early life, fam-
     ily, and his attitude toward writing ("I'm just an old-
     fashioned writer."). Includes a paragraph on the genesis
     of Mr. Sammler's Planet.

21   EPSTEIN, JOSEPH. Review of Mr. Sammler's Planet. Book World
     (1 February), pp. 1, 3.
         Although Mr. Sammler's Planet is likely to offend many
     categories of the reading public, it is a brilliant book.
     Bellow, the most intellectual of our novelists, remains
     unsurpassed at cityscapes and a range of human behavior.
     He continues to be concerned with where we are going, what
     are the consequences of our preoccupations, and what it all
     means.

22   FLETCHER, JANET. Review of Mr. Sammler's Planet. Library
     Journal, 95 (1 February), 511.
         Mr. Sammler's Planet reflects Bellow's difficult strug-
     gle to come to terms with an appalling decade. Sammler is
     a figure without personal desires, one who communicates a
     saving truth. While the book ends balanced between opti-
     mism and despair, it is clear that Bellow again in this
     novel leans toward optimism--toward life and a humanistic
     life force.

23   FOSSUM, ROBERT H. "Inflationary Trends in the Criticism of
     Fiction: Four Studies of Saul Bellow." Studies in the
     Novel, 2 (Spring), 99-104.
         A review article on four studies of Bellow: Tony
     Tanner's Saul Bellow, Keith Opdahl's The Novels of Saul
     Bellow: An Introduction, John Clayton's Saul Bellow: In
     Defense of Man, and Irving Malin's Saul Bellow's Fiction.
     Fossum wonders whether Bellow's work thus far warrants such
     detailed attention; but of these works he finds Tanner's to
     be best: he does "not commit the currently common error of
     confusing fiction with the kind of complex poetry which
     rightfully demands 'close analysis.'" Opdahl's book is
     brilliant in spots, but the details are sometimes more dis-
     tracting than enlightening. Clayton's judgments are acute,

1970

but his examination too microscopic and inflated. Malin's style is clumsy and his conclusions grandiose.

24   FULLER, EDMUND. "Bellow's New Orbit." Wall Street Journal, 175 (30 January), 8.
      Bellow's finest novel, Mr. Sammler's Planet is a universal book, involving us all in the world we share and what we make of it. The book is a witty one, original in invention and conception, and critical of the mood and tone of life today.

25   GERSTENBERGER, DONNA, and GEORGE HENDRICKS. The American Novel: A Checklist of Twentieth Century Criticism on Novels Written since 1789. Vol. II: Criticism Written, 1960-68. Chicago: The Swallow Press.
      Pages 20-26 contain a bibliography on the criticism of Bellow.

26   GRAY, PAUL E. Review of Mr. Sammler's Planet. Yale Review, 59 (Spring), 432-433.
      Bellow's novel is full of "narrative acrobatics." He crams far too many actions and events in so short a time; while he is adept at evoking sensory qualities of experience, he is careless in matching these to the larger pattern of the novel.

27   GROSS, BEVERLY. "The Dark Side of the Moon." Nation, 210 (9 February), 153-55.
      Mr. Sammler's Planet is an "old man's book," with a hero more passive than any of Bellow's earlier heroes. Sammler is finally "less a character than a perspective for viewing the lunacy of our age." Bellow moralizes too much in the novel, denying the novel a dramatic life of its own. "The novel is rich with ideas about life, poor with life itself."

28   GROSS, JOHN. "First and Last Things." The Observer (12 July), p. 25.
      In Mr. Sammler's Planet Bellow displays "his ability to weld together the play of ideas with the ironies of circumstance." Although Sammler appears somewhat "constricted," the minor characters are brilliantly drawn. The long dialogue between Sammler and Govindi Lal is especially well done, and its dramatic function in the novel is effective. On the whole, the novel, which is concerned primarily with first and last things, is rich and satisfying.

29   GROSSMAN, EDWARD. "The Bitterness of Saul Bellow." Midstream, 16 (August-September), 3-15.

Mr. Sammler's Planet is a departure from Bellow's
earlier writings; this novel seems unusually bitter and
desperately bleak. Its protagonist is complex, but the
reader is not moved very deeply by him. The novel is un-
relieved by comedy, and at its most important moments we
see through Bellow's eyes rather than through Sammler's.
At best, Bellow is perfunctory in carrying out the formal
requirements of plot and character; and Mr. Sammler's Planet
turns out to be the novel-as-morality instructor. Bellow
is still our best writer, but this is not his best book.

30 HABER, LEO. "Saul Bellow's Discourse." Jewish Frontier, 37
    (June), 24-26.
        A review of Mr. Sammler's Planet. Whether Bellow is a
    Jewish novelist is still an important question, since an
    author's center of concern molds his world-view. "The
    Jewish author's characters have only one foot in this
    world...and the other in the grave...." So it is with
    Sammler, who knowing the terms of his contract, continues
    to engage in constant talk, speculation, and meditation on
    the human condition.

31 HICKS, GRANVILLE. "Saul Bellow," in Literary Horizons - A
    Quarter Century of American Fiction. New York: New York
    University Press, pp. 49-63.
        Reprints reviews of The Adventures of Augie March
    (1953.B12), Seize the Day (1956.B10), Henderson the Rain
    King (1959.B14), and Herzog (1964.B41).

32 HILL, WILLIAM. Review of Mr. Sammler's Planet. America, 122
    (2 May), 478.
        Brief notice. Mr. Sammler's Planet is Bellow's best
    book to date, showing a man who recognizes all the calls
    which require important human responses.

33 HOWARD, JANE. "Mr. Bellow Considers His Planet." Life, 68
    (3 April), 57-60.
        A profile of Bellow by a writer who spent time with him
    on several different occasions--at a Yale student literary
    gathering and in and about Chicago. Bellow comments on the
    need to "try to redeem" civilization, on the lack of an
    avant-garde, on the lack of novels of ideas, on the younger
    generation, on his travels, and his writings.

34 HOWE, IRVING. Review of Mr. Sammler's Planet. Harper's
    Magazine, 240 (February), 106.
        In this novel, the upper West Side of New York becomes
    transformed "into a principle of sorts, a mixture of health

and sickness exemplifying our condition." The novel is
filled with lively characters and brilliant episodes, but
all is barely held together by the weak unity of action
and theme. The key to that unity is found in the last
paragraph of the book.

35 HUGHES, CATHARINE. "Our Crazy Species." Progressive, 34
(May), 49-50.
Mr. Sammler's Planet, an often tedious, boring novel,
exists "primarily to provide Mr. Sammler with the oppor-
tunity for periodic reflection on the state of man and the
state of the world." The result is unrewarding, the characters unbelievable, the "300 page lecture-demonstration"
unstimulating.

36 JONES, DAVID R. "The Disappointments of Maturity: Bellow's
The Adventures of Augie March," in The Fifties: Fiction,
Poetry, Drama. Edited by Warren French. Deland, Fla.:
Everett Edwards, pp. 83-92.
In this unsympathetic treatment of the novel, Jones
criticizes Bellow's bloated prose, inconsistent style,
vacillating characterizations, and, above all, his vague
imagination.

37 KAZIN, ALFRED. "Though He Slay Me...." New York Review of
Books, 15, No. 10 (3 December), 3.
Of all Jewish novelists, Bellow seems "the most respon-
sive, the most penetrating, the most unyielding in his
ability to express the extraordinariness of the Jewish
'situation.'" Bellow equates virtue with "thinking well"
rather than with action. Sammler is brilliant and percep-
tive, but rather opaque in his relations with other human
beings. He is always "right," others, their thoughts and
actions, are "wrong." Mr. Sammler's Planet is distinguished
by "the formidable intelligence of its author and the pro-
foundly intellectual wit that has formed Bellow's style."

38 KIELY, ROBERT. Review of Mr. Sammler's Planet. Christian
Science Monitor (5 February), p. 11.
This is Bellow's deepest and most reflective book. It
is about death--the death of a man, a people, and an epoch.
"It is an elegy and a lament, punctuated with refrainlike
appeals for mercy and understanding."

39 LACY, ROBERT. Review of Mosby's Memoirs and Other Stories.
Northwest Review, 10 (Summer), 139-40.
The publication of this book is somewhat disappointing
since the six stories have been published before. The

stories try to be something other than stories; Bellow's
poor use of the "envelope" technique does not provide for
an "interplay between past and present."

40   LEHMANN-HAUPT, CHRISTOPHER.   "The Monotonous Music of the
     Spheres." New York Times (26 January), p. 45.
          Mr. Sammler's Planet is flawed in its action, characteri-
     zation, and language. Sammler's "gravitational pull is in-
     sufficient." The issue in the novel is the future of the
     planet, but it is hard to keep from getting lost in
     Sammler's endless ruminations, and the conclusion of the
     book is "trite and anticlimatic."

41   LINDROTH, JAMES. Review of Mr. Sammler's Planet. America,
     122 (21 February), 190.
          A brief review. In Mr. Sammler's Planet belief gives
     meaning: "Bellow's protagonist believes in the efficacy
     of prayer, the dignity of man, the value of friendship, and
     the primacy of goodness."

42   LODGE, DAVID. Review of Mr. Sammler's Planet. Tablet
     (London), 224 (18 July), 691.
          In this novel Bellow uses his medium as a vehicle for
     thought as well as feeling. "The prose is wonderfully ver-
     satile, stretching to embrace the mundane and the meta-
     physical." Its main weakness is Bellow's "insistent
     presence at Mr. Sammler's elbow," signifying an inability
     to detach himself sufficiently from his hero.

43   LURIE, ALISON. "The View From the Moon." New Statesman, 80
     (10 July), 19.
          A review of Mr. Sammler's Planet. Bellow remains "one
     of the best writers anywhere in the world today." He con-
     tinues to turn experience into literature. Stylistically,
     Bellow is not conservative, but Mr. Sammler's Planet is a
     conservative book: "Sammler's final conclusions are stoi-
     cal, almost pessimistic."

*44 MATHY, FRANCIS. "Zetsubo no kanata ni." Sophia: Studies in
     Western Civilization and the Cultural Interaction of East
     and West (Tokyo), 19 (1970), 356-77.
          An essay in Japanese on the humanism of Saul Bellow and
     John Updike. Cited in Modern Language Association Inter-
     national Bibliography, 1 (1971), 143.

45   MIDWOOD, BARTON. Review of Mr. Sammler's Planet. Esquire,
     74 (December), 96.

1970

Mr. Sammler's Planet should not be read for its thin
plot, but for its honest and engaging characterizations.
Here one finds, in Sammler, Herzog as an old man.

46 MORTON, FREDERIC. Review of Mr. Sammler's Planet. Village
    Voice, 15 (26 February), 7.
        Morton recalls the many Sammler-types he knew in his
    youth. Bellow's Sammler seems authentic, except that "his
    discomfitures don't consume him...he consumes them."
    Sammler processes all of his past into enrichments of his
    consciousness. He is a cold fish, but a lovable one, and
    Bellow's parody of him is "the rare kind which bolsters the
    substance and warmth of the thing parodied."

47 MOSS, JUDITH P. "The Body as Symbol in Saul Bellow's Henderson
    the Rain King." Literature and Psychology, 20 (1970),
    51-61.
        In Henderson the Rain King, "the body of Eugene Henderson,
    viewed in the light of Freudian conversion symptomatology,
    is the central dramatic symbol...which functions in char-
    acterization, shapes the narrative, and metaphorically
    generates the dual theme of regeneration and recovery."

48 OATES, JOYCE C. "Articulations." Critic, 28 (May-June),
    68-69.
        A review of Mr. Sammler's Planet. Sammler's life de-
    pends upon "the careful articulations of a few important
    questions and their tentative answers." Sammler is more
    human than Bellow's earlier heroes, but he is set in the
    middle of a bizarre group of people with whom he must cope.
    And he copes with wisdom and eloquence. Bellow's energetic,
    brilliant writing involves us both intellectually and
    emotionally.

49 OPDAHL, KEITH. Review of Mr. Sammler's Planet. Commonweal,
    91 (13 February), 535.
        While the novel deserves reading for its polished, con-
    trolled style, and for its timely ideas on the present
    state of our culture, it is in many ways disappointing.
    The ideas overshadow the story, Mr. Sammler is too sane,
    and Bellow gets himself "trapped by Sammler's virtues."
    In the early novels, the heroes fear for their sanity; in
    Mr. Sammler's Planet, the secondary characters are mad.

50 PEARCE, RICHARD. Stages of the Clown: Perspectives on Modern
    Fiction from Dostoevsky to Beckett. Carbondale: Southern
    Illinois University Press.

In chapter 7 (pp. 102-116), there is a discussion of the clown as <u>harlequin</u> in <u>Henderson the Rain King</u> and John Hawkes <u>Second Skin</u>.

51 PEARSON, GABRIEL. "Creatureliness." <u>Guardian Weekly</u>, 103 (25 July), 19.
In <u>Mr. Sammler's Planet</u>, as well as in his earlier novels, Bellow's "effort is for the survival of novelistic intelligence as such in a society where all discourse threatens to reduce itself to violence, manipulation, and rape." <u>Mr. Sammler's Planet</u>, at its best, is a "lovely, involuted fable of how we must breathe the poisoned air of our own condition and learn to live off it." At its worst, it is too artful, talkative, and too schematically interconnected.

52 PRITCHARD, WILLIAM. Review of <u>Mr. Sammler's Planet</u>. <u>Hudson Review</u>, 23 (Spring), 169-70.
<u>Mr. Sammler's Planet</u> is "essentially a conservative lament." The novel is sparer, much more concentrated than <u>Herzog</u>. As a very contemporary novel, it leaves us with nothing more than conscience, "the responsibility of being human."

53 RUPP, RICHARD H. "Saul Bellow: Belonging to the World in General." <u>Celebration in Postwar American Fiction, 1945-1967</u>. Coral Gables, Fla.: University of Miami Press, pp. 189-208.
Bellow's novels through <u>Herzog</u> are examined in terms of the experience of celebration. His heroes "celebrate reality in festive approval," and at the heart of their celebration is "the affirmation of life in the face of death."

54 SAMUELS, CHARLES T. "Bellow on Modernism." <u>New Republic</u>, 162 (7 February), 27-30.
<u>Mr. Sammler's Planet</u> is "middling Bellow"--an intelligent novel but one with an "imperfect connection between action and idea." Most impressive in the book are Sammler's monologues, but they do not save the book from being "a sermon designed for the already converted."

55 SISSMAN, L. E. "Uptight." <u>The New Yorker</u>, 45 (31 January), 82, 85, 86-87.
A review of <u>Mr. Sammler's Planet</u>, Bellow's "chief work." The novel is an "implicit defense of human discipline and decency." The genius of the book lies in the choice of the few, catholic characters.

1970

56   SOKOLOV, RAYMOND A.   Review of Mr. Sammler's Planet.   Newsweek,
     75 (2 February), 77.
          Rivaling anything he has done for "sheer splendor of
     prose," Mr. Sammler's Planet is yet difficult to take seri-
     ously. "Those jeweled cadances, that stylish simian meta-
     phor, that measured, careful, extended verbosity, all take
     the edge off Sammler's (or is it Bellow's?) basic point."
     Bellow has overreacted; his tone is bitter.

57   STOCK, IRWIN.   "Man in Culture."   Commentary, 49 (May), 89-94.
          Mr. Sammler's Planet is Bellow's way of showing that
     man's sense of himself as a free, precious individual can
     easily be caricaturized and vulgarized in today's society.
     The book is thus arranged as a series of confrontations
     between Sammler, the humanist, and "a group of characters
     chosen to represent the current Zeitgeist." The mere asser-
     tion of individuality "debases the self it seeks to glorify."
     In this novel as in his others, Bellow promotes the claims
     and standards of our common humanity; he is "pre-eminently
     the novelist of man-in-culture."

58   SULLIVAN, WALTER.   "Where Have All the Flowers Gone?"   Sewanee
     Review, 78 (Autumn), 654-64.
          In this review article on several recent novels, Sullivan
     finds Mr. Sammler's Planet (pp. 662-64) a work achieving
     dignity. "Sammler is a proper image of modern man, a true
     rendition of what we are in our fragmentation and indecision
     and alienation." A deep sickness infects our age, and
     Sammler can properly allow himself only a "small affirmation."

59   TUBE, HENRY.   "Poisoned Wells."   Spectator (18 July), p. 44.
          Mr. Sammler's Planet, a good novel (or possibly a good
     sermon) is a kind of melancholy, hopeful plea for sanity in
     a mad world. The novel moves in the direction of redemp-
     tion, and the redemptive urge in Bellow tends to distort
     and oversimplify the real world. "Mr. Sammler himself lacks
     edges," so, while we respect him, we learn little of our-
     selves from him.

60   WALLENSTEIN, BARRY.   "Mad, Mad World."   Catholic World
     (September), p. 275.
          Mr. Sammler's Planet is a "guided tour of the absurdity,
     chaos, and beauty that is our contemporary civilization."
     Mr. Sammler has accumulated experience and knowledge which
     enable him to view the world objectively. As an old man,
     Sammler is "not a model of what is passé or outmoded, but
     of our salvation."

61 WEINBERG, HELEN. The New Novel in America: The Kafkan Mode
    in Contemporary Fiction. Ithaca, New York: Cornell Uni-
    versity Press.
        Chapter 3 of this book is on "Kafka and Bellow: Com-
    parisons and Further Definitions," and chapter 4 is on "The
    Heroes of Saul Bellow's Novels." Like Kafka, Bellow has a
    commitment to literature for the sake of life, his own and
    others, rather than for the sake of art or ideology. For
    him literature is a form of inquiry, and, as in Kafka, the
    personal in his novels becomes inevitably metaphysical and
    spiritual. Bellow's heroes can be seen as either victims,
    activists, or sufferers; in a Kafkan pattern their inner
    life is manifest through surface action. These heroes are
    on metaphysical quests in pursuit of a truth about the self
    "that only the past, rather than the present-toward-the-
    future may reveal...."

62 WISSE, RUTH R. "The Schlemihl as Hero in Yiddish and American
    Fiction." Ph.D. dissertation, McGill University. Listed
    in Dissertation Abstracts International, 30 (7: January),
    2983A.
        Yiddish story tellers have used the schlemihl hero "to
    explore the irony of a faith which could coexist with
    doubt." American Jewish writers, particularly Malamud and
    Bellow, have used the schlemihl-hero "to explore the para-
    dox of failure as success within a secular humanist culture."

1971 A BOOKS

1   DUTTON, ROBERT R. Saul Bellow. New York: Twayne Publishers,
    177 pp.
        This study of Bellow's novels is based on the theme of
    man as a subangelic being. In devoting a chapter to each
    of the novels through Herzog, Dutton seeks to answer the
    question, "If Bellow the essayist prescribes a turning away
    from past definitions of experience, what precisely does
    Bellow the novelist substitute for those definitions?" The
    final chapter presents an overview and assessment of Bellow,
    with a consideration of the thematic patterns in his novels;
    his technical and stylistic skills as they are seen in his
    use of characterization, distance, and point of view; his
    role as a humorist and as an urban novelist; and his stand-
    ing with regard to contemporary American literature. There
    is a brief supplementary chapter on Mr. Sammler's Planet,
    and a selected bibliography, pp. 169-77.

1971

2   SOKOLOFF, B. A., and MARK E. POSNER. Saul Bellow: A Comprehensive Bibliography. Folcroft, Pa.: Folcroft Press,
49 pp.
A limited edition (150 copies) bibliography of primary
sources (books, short fiction, articles, reviews, interviews) and secondary sources (reviews, books, biographical
material, and general criticism). There are no
annotations.

1971 B SHORTER WRITINGS

1   BRAEM, HELMUT M. "Der Weg Saul Bellows." Neue Rundschau,
82 (Part 2, No. 4), 742-52.
A general survey, in German, of Bellow's novels, with
special emphasis on Mr. Sammler's Planet.

2   BUFITHIS, PHILIP H. "The Artist's Fight for Art: The Psychi-
atrist Figure in the Fiction of Major Contemporary Ameri-
can Novelists." Ph.D. dissertation, University of
Pennsylvania, 269 pp. Listed in Dissertation Abstracts
International, 32 (4: October), 2083A (Order No. 71-25,987).
Chapters on eight American novelists: Nabakov,
W. Burroughs, Bellow, Salinger, Mailer, Barth, Purdy, and
Kesey. Among these novelists, the psychiatrist is a char-
acter against whom the artist-protagonist defines himself.
As a steward of the Reality Principle, the psychiatrist
threatens the values which the artist attempts to create
for himself.

3   CHAPMAN, SARA S. "Melville and Bellow in the Real World:
Pierre and Augie March." West Virginia University Philo-
logical Papers, 18 (September), 51-57.
There are many similarities of perspective between The
Adventures of Augie March and Pierre: both novels share
an idealistic vision of the hero's initial response to the
world, and both present a youthful tragedy as their heroes
"become immersed in the ambiguities of the world they discover." In this world there are no set standards of ethics
or morality. Melville and Bellow see the world characterized by the dialectical, with its only constancy to be
found in change and process.

*4   CORNIS-POP, MARCEL. "Alienarea si necesitatea reintegrarii in
societate: Consideratii asupra romanului lui Saul Bellow."
Orizont: Revista a Uniunii Scriitorilor din R. S. Romania,
22 (v), 51-57.
Cited in Modern Language Association International
Bibliography, 1 (1971), 143.

5   DRABBLE, MARGARET. "A Myth to Stump the Experts." New
    Statesman, 81 (26 March), 435.
        An enthusiastic review of Henderson the Rain King which
    renews the writer's faith in the modern novel as a living,
    vital form. This novel is Bellow's "funniest, his least
    misogynist, and his least overworked, and it is written in
    a prose so beautiful and vivid and immediate that it leaves
    one breathless."

6   EPSTEIN, JOSEPH. "Saul Bellow of Chicago." New York Times
    Book Review (9 May), pp. 4, 12, 14, 16.
        Bellow is acknowledged as the premier American novelist,
    one who has built up a carefully developed body of work,
    but one who is hardly recognized in the non-literary
    Chicago. In a conversation with Epstein, Bellow comments
    on his favorite novelists, the difficulty of writing good
    fiction today, the demands Americans place on their writers,
    and those who are "publicity intellectuals."

7   GROSS, THEODORE L. "Saul Bellow: The Victim and the Hero,"
    in The Heroic Ideal in American Literature. New York:
    Free Press, pp. 243-61.
        In discussing the novels through Herzog, Gross shows
    that Bellow rejects a traditional heroism and instead ex-
    presses a genuine radicalism that makes idealism humanly
    credible. His heroes are suffering victims who direct
    their suffering toward love, salvation, and self-perception.
    Their suffering ultimately issues "in moderate idealism, in
    muted comic affirmation."

8   GUTTMANN, ALLEN. "Mr. Bellow's America." The Jewish Writer
    in America: Assimilation and the Crisis of Identity.
    New York: Oxford University Press, pp. 178-221.
        A discussion of each of the novels through Mr. Sammler's
    Planet. Bellow is found to be the par excellence "explorer
    of marginality, concerned with men situated somewhere be-
    tween old and new, with comic and tragic characters in
    quest of their uncertain identities."

*9 HADARI, AMNON. "Ha-professor Eino Me'uban: Cohav Halekhet
    Shel Mar Sammler Me'et Saul Bellow." Shdemot, 44 (1971),
    102-13.
        Cited in Modern Language Association International
    Bibliography, 1 (1971), 143.

10 HANDY, WILLIAM J. Modern Fiction: A Formalist Approach.
    Carbondale: Southern Illinois University Press.

1971

Chapter 6 is on Seize the Day. Seize the Day is an important novel for it shows Tommy's "attempt to discover and evaluate himself at first in terms of the values he held while growing up and the effect these values had on his present situation and then in terms of his present values and present relationships." The image of Tommy expresses a confidence in the basic nature of man who is caught in the dehumanizing forces of mid-twentieth-century existence.

11   HARPER, H. M., JR. Review of Mr. Sammler's Planet. Contemporary Literature, 12 (Spring), 211.
The tone of Mr. Sammler's Planet is elegiac, and the subject of the elegy "may be the human history of the Earth itself." The book is concerned with the "directions and dimensions of human evolution," and with the necessity to accept anew our human responsibilities in this evolution.

12   HAYS, PETER L. The Limping Hero: Grotesques in Literature. New York: New York University Press, pp. 55-59.
Briefly examines Bellow's use of fertility myth material ("half in earnest and half in joke") in "A Sermon by Doctor Pep" and Henderson the Rain King.

13   HILL, JOHN S. "The Letters of Moses Herzog: A Symbolic Mirror." Studies in the Humanities, 2 (Summer), 40-45.
In Bellow's later novels environment plays a smaller and smaller role. In Herzog, Bellow gives "far more emphasis to its role as a reflection of the hero's thought, and far less to its power to affect him." Through the writing of letters, Herzog comes to self-realization; as an individual he is not a victim of his environment but can "reconstruct the world in his own image so that he may realize his own individuality."

14   HULL, BYRON D. "Henderson the Rain King and William James." Criticism, 13 (Fall), 402-14.
The chapters in Henderson the Rain King dealing with Henderson, Dahfu, and Atti are explicable in terms of Jamesian psychology. Dahfu "functions as a psychotherapist, employing the ideas of James' Psychology in a program of rehabilitation." Parallels in James' Psychology can be found in Dahfu's diagnosis of Henderson's condition, the program he develops to open Henderson's mental channels, and the course of his treatment; further parallels can be found as Henderson draws upon resources of his will, faces up to a supreme test, discovers his latent possibilities, and develops his spiritual self.

15   JOSIPOVICI, GABRIEL. "Bellow and Herzog." Encounter, 37
      (November), 49-55.
         As the novel proceeds, Herzog achieves a greater aware-
      ness of the need to reject two false extremes, represented
      by the terms "potatoe love" and "crisis ethics." Herzog
      finds that he must avoid the structure that these two ex-
      tremes impose: "to give shape to the feelings of the heart
      is to falsify the experience." Bellow has "succeeded in
      constructing a work which is an attack on the structuring
      activity of the mind."

16   KAZIN, ALFRED. "Midtown and the Village." Harper's Magazine,
      242 (January), 82-89.
         In discussing writers he had met in New York during the
      War Years, Kazin found Bellow to be a young writer with a
      vocation, one whose convictions and sense of destiny im-
      pressed all who met him. He "loosened the bonds of ideol-
      ogy for the rest of us." He was "in touch," with an
      unusual inner freedom.

17   KNOKE, PAUL D. "The Allegorical Mode in the Contemporary
      American Novel of Romance." Ph.D. dissertation, Ohio
      University. Listed in Dissertation Abstracts International,
      32 (5: November), 2695A (Order No. 71-29,532).
         Allegory is explored in relation to four contemporary
      novels, including Henderson the Rain King. By allegory in
      the novel is meant "a narrative mode in which the author
      consciously shapes theme and structure by portraying char-
      acter and depicting event in the perspective of an indepen-
      dent frame of reference, both levels working together in
      what might be termed a metaphor of purpose."

18   LEBOWITZ, NAOMI. Humanism and the Absurd in the Modern Novel.
      Evanston, Ill.: Northwestern University Press, pp. 117-22.
         A brief examination of the "satanic debate" in The
      Victim.

*19   LePELLEC, YVES. "New York in Summer: Its Symbolical Function
      in The Victim." Caliban (Toulouse), 8 (1971), 101-10.
         Cited in Modern Language Association International
      Bibliography, 1 (1971), 143.

20   LOCKE, RICHARD. "The Last Word: Two Old Men." New York Times
      Book Review (3 October), p. 47.
         A comparison of Mr. Sammler's Planet and Edmund Wilson's
      Upstate, two books which center on the figure of an old man.

1971

21   LUTWACK, LEONARD. Heroic Fiction: The Epic Tradition and
      American Novels of the Twentieth Century. Carbondale:
      Southern Illinois University Press, pp. 88-121.
          In Chapter 5 Lutwack examines four novels, Seize the
      Day, Henderson the Rain King, Herzog, and Mr. Sammler's
      Planet, to show how Bellow repeatedly uses the metaphor of
      the journey of Odysseus as each of his heroes try to dis-
      cover enough to continue living in a time of personal and
      public crisis.

22   MAJDIAK, DANIEL. "The Romantic Self and Henderson the Rain
      King." Bucknell Review, 19 (Fall), 125-46.
          In Henderson the Rain King Bellow explores his theme of
      the place of the self in modern society in terms of the
      concept of the self derived from Romanticism. Bellow is
      concerned that accepting the loss of the self may help
      destroy belief in the power and value of the imagination.
      In the novel Bellow alludes to Blake, Wordsworth, Shelley,
      and Coleridge to develop his theme.

23   MARKOS, DONALD W. "Life Against Death in Henderson the Rain
      King." Modern Fiction Studies, 17: 193-205.
          Henderson is both a victim and a representative of the
      spiritual madness of modern American society; he maintains
      a view of man's alienated state, but insists that this is
      only a transitional condition. In Africa he confronts the
      realities of his own nature, and in Dahfu sees the possi-
      bility of an organically unified existence, the ideal of
      the "natural" man. In his return to America, though, he
      achieves a more distinctly human re-integration of his
      personality.

24   MOSHER, HAROLD F., JR. "The Synthesis of Past and Present in
      Saul Bellow's Herzog." Wascana Review, 6 (i), 28-38.
          This novel is read as a "philosophical dialogue between
      the Herzog of the present--a Herzog gaining in self-
      awareness--and the Herzog of the past--a Herzog...mostly
      ignorant of his mistakes." As he comes to understand the
      past and its relevance to the present, he is able to change
      his attitude toward life.

25   PINSKER, SANFORD. "The Psychological Schlemiels of Saul
      Bellow," in The Schlemiel as Metaphor: Studies in the
      Yiddish and American Jewish Novel. Carbondale: Southern
      Illinois University Press, pp. 125-57.
          A revision of a dissertation, 1968.B15. Joseph,
      Leventhal, Tommy Wilhelm, and Herzog can be considered
      schlemiels in that they tend to will their own failure.

As introspective dangling men, these heroes are psychological schlemiels, men "whose failures are of the spirit
rather than reversals of the marketplace."

*26 RAO, R. M. V. R. "Chaos of the Self: An Approach to Saul
     Bellow's Dangling Man." Osmania Journal of English Studies,
     8 (ii), 89-103.
         Cited in Modern Language Association International
     Bibliography, 1 (1972), 153.

27   RODRIGUES, EUSEBIO L. "Bellow's Africa." American Literature,
     43 (May), 242-56.
         Bellow utilizes a knowledge of anthropology, particularly
     African ethnography, in Henderson the Rain King. His novel
     reflects the work of anthropologists Melville Herskovits
     and John Roscoe, and of the nineteenth-century travel
     writers Frederick Forbes and Richard Burton. Burton's A
     Mission to Gelele the King of Dahomey, in particular, pro-
     vided him with a model for the creation of King Dahfu, his
     court, and the Wariri. Bellow also made use of details from
     from Roscoe's books on Central Africa for descriptions of
     the natives and their ceremonies. Despite these influences
     and borrowings, Bellow's Africa is "an astonishing feat of
     creative synthesis." It is a "world complete unto it-
     self,...an alchemic fusion of Bellow's anthropological
     reading, his inventive skill, and his imaginative daring
     as a novelist."

*28 SATYANARAYANA, M. R. "The Reality Teacher as Hero: A Study
     of Mr. Sammler's Planet." Osmania Journal of English
     Studies, 8 (ii), 55-68.
         Cited in Modern Language Association International
     Bibliography, 1 (1972), 154.

29   SCHEER-SCHÄZLER, BRIGITTE. "Die Farbe als dichterisches
     Gestaltungsmittel in den Romanen Saul Bellows." Die
     Sprachkunst, 2 (1971), 243-64.
         An essay, in German, on the use of color as a poetic
     device in the novels of Bellow. The appearances of color
     are cited, as well as the use of color in designations,
     comparisons, metaphors, and symbols, and its achievement in
     establishing rhythms, characterization, intensity, con-
     creteness, transcendence, and ambivalence.

*30 SCHUELER, MARY D. "The Figure of Madeleine in Herzog." Notes
     on Contemporary Literature, 1 (iii), 5-7.
         Cited in Modern Language Association International
     Bibliography, 1 (1971), 143.

Writings about Saul Bellow, 1944-1976

1971

*31   SHASTRI, N. R. "Self and Society in Saul Bellow's The Victim." Osmania Journal of English Studies, 8 (ii), 105-12.
Cited in Modern Language Association International Bibliography, 1 (1972), 154.

32   TANNER, TONY. City of Words: American Fiction, 1950-70. New York: Harper and Row, pp. 64-73, 295-310.
Chapters 3 and 15 are devoted in part to Bellow. In his discussion, Tanner emphasizes the "mode of motion" in The Adventures of Augie March and the pattern of fictionalized recall in Herzog.

*33   TOTH, SUSAN. "Henderson the Rain King, Eliot and Browning." Notes on Contemporary Literature, 1 (v), 6-8.
Cited in Modern Language Association International Bibliography, 1 (1971), 143.

34   USTVEDT, YNGVAR. "Saul Bellow--en Amerikansk Nåtidsdikter." Samtiden, 80 (1971), 273-82.
An essay, in Norwegian, on Bellow as a significant contemporary American writer.

35   WATERMAN, ANDREW. "Saul Bellow's Ineffectual Angels," in On the Novel: A Present for Walter Allen on His 60th Birthday from His Friends and Colleagues. Edited by B. S. Benedikz. London: Dent, pp. 218-39.
The novels through Mr. Sammler's Planet are examined to demonstrate Bellow's mastery of prose style, of comedy, of the imaginative process, and of theme. Bellow's characters are considered to be ineffectual angels--men who "have failed in a hostile world to realize their aspirations towards some goodness achieved within human fellowship."

1972 A BOOKS

1   INGLEHART, BABETTE. Drama As Reality and Metaphor in the Work of Saul Bellow. Ph.D. dissertation, The University of Chicago.
Cited in Comprehensive Dissertation Index, 1861-1972, 35: 155.

2   MERKOWITZ, DAVID R. "Bellow's Early Phase: Self and Society in Dangling Man, The Victim, and The Adventures of Augie March." Ph.D. dissertation, University of Michigan, 263 pp. Listed in Dissertation Abstracts International, 32 (11: May), 6439A-40A (Order No. 72-14,943).

116

Writings about Saul Bellow, 1944-1976

Bellow's early phase "is characterized initially by a rather closed form and a narrowness of focus, and is capped by a sudden release into open form and broad experience." Bellow uses these forms to explore the existential process by which the individual comes to grasp his own identity in the context of an alien society.

3   SCHEER-SCHÄZLER, BRIGITTE. Saul Bellow. New York: Ungar, 150 pp.
      This study of the novels focuses on the attempts of Bellow's characters to know themselves amid the pressures and confusions of American life, and their attempts to understand the extent to which they have freedom as individuals and have the ability to improve their human condition. The first chapter, "The Price of Release," is devoted to Dangling Man and The Victim; chapter 2, "Bitterness is his Chosen Thing," to The Adventures of Augie March; chapter 3, "The Dread is Great, the Soul is Small," to Seize the Day; chapter 4, "Every Guy Has His Own Africa," to Henderson the Rain King; chapter 5, "History, Memory—That Is What Makes Us Human," to Herzog; and chapter 6, "The Benefit of an Enlarged Vision," to Mr. Sammler's Planet.

1972 B SHORTER WRITINGS

1   ADELMAN, IRVING, and RITA DIVORKIN. The Contemporary Novel: A Checklist of Critical Literature on the British and American Novel since 1945. Metuchen, N. J.: Scarecrow Press.
      Pages 46-59 contain a bibliography on Bellow.

2   ALDRIDGE, JOHN. The Devil in the Fire: Retrospective Essays on American Literature and Culture, 1951-1971. New York: Harper's Magazine Press.
      Reprints "The Complacency of Herzog" (pp. 231-34): 1962.B2; and "The Society of Augie March" (pp. 224-30): 1956.B1.

3   BAKKER, J. "In Search of Reality: Two American Heroes Compared." Dutch Quarterly Review of Anglo-American Letters, 4 (1972), 145-61.
      A comparison of the similarities and differences of Hemingway and Bellow heroes. In common they have "their need to solve the problem of identity in a society that no longer provides readymade answers." They differ in their approaches to a solution. Hemingway's heroes place themselves outside the community of men, while Bellow's heroes have their actions determined by their relationships with fellowmen.

1972

*4 BALOTĂ, NICOLAE. "Saul Bellow şi romanul inadăptarii."
    România Literară, 5:31, 27 (July), 13.
        An essay on Saul Bellow and the "novel of misfitting."
    Cited in Modern Language Association International Bibliog-
    raphy, 1 (1972), 153.

5   CECIL, L. MOFFITT. "Bellow's Henderson as American Imago of
    the 1950's." Research Studies (Washington State Univer-
    sity), 40 (December), 296-300.
        Henderson projects an affirmative image of the America
    of the 1950's—"The awakening giant, on the verge of a new
    consciousness, representing the hopes and determinations of
    those who still share the American dream...." The back-
    ground of Henderson, and the separate events during his
    pilgrimage, help support the thesis that he has been devel-
    oped as the personification of a newly emerging American
    consciousness.

6   FINKELSTEIN, SIDNEY. "The Anti-Hero of Updike, Bellow and
    Malamud." American Dialog, 7 (Spring), 12-14, 30.
        Mr. Sammler, whom Bellow makes "a daring Freethinker,"
    is one of the anti-heroes who appears to be taking over
    American literature. Mr. Sammler's Planet is a dense,
    pseudo-intellectual novel which reveals Bellow's distortion
    and misinterpretation of Marx. It is "an expertly written
    but fraudulent, bad racist novel, which serves the very
    elements in civilization it pretends to despise."

7   FRIEDMAN, ALAN W. "The Jews Complaint in Recent American
    Fiction: Beyond Exodus and Still in the Wilderness."
    Southern Review, 8 (Winter), 41-59.
        The Jew in America continues to seek assimilation into
    the culture; regardless of the degree of his success, the
    alienation he feels is not unusual since alienation is a
    common, deeply American theme. Jewish writers like Bellow,
    Malamud, and Roth claim the maligned Jewish stereotype as
    their own, and they "create characters whose verbal vitality
    invigorates a still-significant wrestling with heritage and
    cultural context."

8   GOLDEN, DANIEL. "Shapes and Strategies: Forms of Modern
    American Fiction in the Novels of Robert Penn Warren, Saul
    Bellow, and John Barth." Ph.D. dissertation, Indiana Uni-
    versity, 225 pp. Listed in Dissertation Abstracts Inter-
    national, 33 (6: December), 2933A-34A (Order No. 72-30,410).
        In adopting formal strategies, each of these authors tend
    to utilize the conventions and traditions of certain fic-
    tional subgenres; Bellow's fiction is indebted to the

tradition of the confessional novel, which begins with
Dostoevsky. His central characters are confessor figures,
"whose movement from alienation to accommodation with self
and society is based on their ability to comprehend the
implications of their own confessions."

9 HARRIS, JAMES N. "One Critical Approach to Mr. Sammler's
   Planet." Twentieth Century Literature, 18 (1972), 235-50.
        In Bellow's development as a novelist, Mr. Sammler's
   Planet reveals a shift from an ethical base to a religious
   faith, and a return to the mythic mode from the ironic.
   With sardonic humor, Bellow parodies elements of his previous work within this novel. Near its end, Sammler becomes Bellow's persona, and the real thrust of the novel
   is shown--the revelation of God through a new pronouncement
   of Logos.

*10 HEINEY, DONALD. "Bellow as European," in Modern American Fic-
   tion: Insights and Foreign Lights. Proceedings of the
   Comparative Literature Symposium, Volume 5. Interdepart-
   mental Committee on Comparative Literature. Lubbock:
   Texas Technical University, pp. 77-88.
        Cited in Modern Language Association International
   Bibliography, 1 (1972), 153.

11 HONMA, NAGAYO. "Saul Bellow no Gendai Bunka Ron." Eigo
   Seinen (Tokyo), 118 (1972), 260-61.
        An essay, in Japanese, on Saul Bellow and contemporary
   American culture.

12 IWAMOTO, IWAO. "Judea-kei Sakka no Miryoku--Bellow to
   Malamud." Eigo Seinen (Tokyo), 118 (1972), 257-60.
        An essay, in Japanese, on the appeal of the Jewish
   writers, Bellow and Malamud.

13 IWAYAMA, TAJIRO. "Marginal Man no ikiru Joken--Saul Bellow no
   Herzog to Mr. Sammler's Planet." Eigo Seinen (Tokyo), 118
   (1972), 133-35.
        An essay, in Japanese, on the conditions for life of a
   modern "marginal" man, as represented in Herzog and
   Mr. Sammler's Planet.

14 KULSHRESTHA, CHIRANTAN. "A Conversation with Saul Bellow."
   Chicago Review, 23-24 (1972), 7-15.
        A transcribed conversation with Bellow that took place
   January 12, 1971. Bellow discusses the novel of ideas, the
   difficulty of representing "good men" in fiction, the
   affirmation of his characters, the novelist and the media,

1972

the authority of the writer, his writing of Seize the Day
and The Adventures of Augie March, and the relationship of
his Jewishness to his writing.

15 KUNA, F. M. "The European Culture Game: Mr. Bellow's Planet."
English Studies, 53 (1972), 531-44.
    An essay on Mr. Sammler's Planet, which is considered to
be a brilliant, timely novel. Sammler has a paradoxical
nature: "on the one hand he longs for the purity, simplic-
ity, impersonality of the Platonic universe and Augustinian
theology, on the other he does not accept these things as
given truths." Sammler "wants to reach his timeless goal
by individual striving, by a continuous process of exploration and self-discovery, by a permanent state of intellectual excitement and endeavor." While the Mr. Sammler's
Planet is brilliant and timely, as a novel it fails; it is
in many ways a long essay with symbols and plot structures
thrown in later. It revives the well-established tradition
of moralizing, destroying an instinctive, mysterious center
of the book, and reversing the negative and positive poles
in any dialectical scheme.

16 LOFROTH, ERIK. "Herzog's Predicament: Saul Bellow's View of
Modern Man." Studia Neophilologica, 44 (1972), 315-25.
    A study of Herzog's predicament in relation to three
influences: his past Jewish experiences, his American
environment, and his studies. In the novel there is an
interplay between the influences on Herzog as a Jew and
Herzog as a scholar.

17 MILLER, NORMAN. "The Self-Conscious Narrator-Protagonist in
American Fiction Since World War II." Ph.D. dissertation,
University of Wisconsin, 229 pp. Listed in Dissertation
Abstracts International, 32 (10: April), 5798A (Order No.
72-9140).
    This is a study of the self-conscious narrator-
protagonist in novels by Salinger, Bellow, Vonnegut,
Nabokov, Barth, Ellison, Cozzens, Hawkes, Oates, and Roth.
In Bellow's Dangling Man there is an excellent example of
the self-conscious narrator-protagonist: Joseph is both
the subject and vehicle of his story, and "because his
aims are fundamentally rhetorical, he is, to some extent,
unreliable."

18 NELSON, GERALD B. "Tommy Wilhelm." Ten Versions of America.
New York: Knopf, pp. 129-45.
    A consideration of Tommy Wilhelm as one of ten repre-
sentative types in contemporary fiction who are in pursuit
of the American dream.

19   NEVIUS, BLAKE. "Saul Bellow and the Theater of the Soul."
     Neuphilologische Mitteilungen, 73 (i-ii), 248-60.
          An essay focusing primarily on Mr. Sammler's Planet.
     Sammler "becomes the vehicle not only of Bellow's skepti-
     cism, which he shares with his age, but of his persistent
     if rather desperate optimism." In attempting to determine
     how a good man should live, Sammler finds an answer in the
     character and history of Elya Gruner. By comparing the
     Atlantic Monthly version of Mr. Sammler's Planet (which
     preceded the publication of the novel by several months)
     to the novel, one can see in Bellow's revisions what a
     central function in the novel Gruner is intended to play.

*20 PORTER, M. GILBERT. "Henderson the Rain King: An Orchestra-
     tion of Soul Music." New England Review, 1, 6 (Spring),
     24-33.
          Cited in Porter, p. 206: 1974.A3.

21   SAEKI, SHOICHI. "An Hour With Saul Bellow." Eigo Seinen
     (Tokyo), 118 (1972), 246-53.
          An important wide-ranging interview, in English, during
     which Bellow discusses his association with universities,
     the function of universities in supporting humanists, the
     humanist as rebel, the isolation of Americans and writers
     in particular, the professionalism of literary studies,
     and didacticism in contemporary American literature.

22   SALTER, D. P. M. "Optimism and Reaction in Saul Bellow's
     Recent Work." Critical Quarterly, 14 (Spring), 57-66.
          In Mr. Sammler's Planet Bellow explores the qualities
     that Herzog was only groping for at the end of his novel:
     sanctity, wholeness, self-knowledge. But Sammler becomes
     too much a mouthpiece for Bellow's ideas. Too often Bellow
     portrays him without irony as a man who lacks emotion. The
     novel is fundamentally ambivalent since Bellow has not suf-
     ficiently distanced himself from his hero.

*23 SASTRI, P. S. "Bellow's Henderson the Rain King: A Quest for
     Being." Punjab University Research Bulletin (Arts), 3 (i),
     9-18.
          Cited in Modern Language Association International
     Bibliography, 1 (1972), 154.

24   SHIBUYA, YUSABURO. "Saul Bellow Ron--Moralist to shite no
     Sokumen wo Chushin ni." Eigo Seinen (Tokyo), 118 (1972),
     254-56.
          A study of Saul Bellow centering on the moralistic
     aspects of his writings. In Japanese.

1972

25 WARNER, STEPHEN D. "Representative Studies in the American
    Picaresque: Investigations of <u>Modern Chivalry</u>, <u>Adventures
    of Huckleberry Finn</u>, and <u>The Adventures of Augie March</u>."
    Ph.D. dissertation, Indiana University, 195 pp. Listed in
    <u>Dissertation Abstracts International</u>, 32 (8: February),
    4582A (Order No. 72-6843).
        By considering Spanish prototypes of the picaresque,
    this study defines the picaro "as vehicle, vision, and
    voice in a narrative which emphasizes, illuminates, and
    usually undercuts, the society around him." Augie March
    performs all of these functions of the traditional picaro.

1973 A BOOKS

1   KAR, PARFULLA C. "Saul Bellow: A Defense of the Self."
    Ph.D. dissertation, University of Utah, 186 pp. Listed in
    <u>Dissertation Abstracts International</u>, 34 (August), 778A
    (Order No. 73-19,365).
        Bellow's primary concern as a novelist is to uphold and
    defend man's sovereign self amidst the social and techno-
    logical dislocations of this century. The first chapter
    discusses Bellow's various writings on the dignity of the
    self; subsequent chapters discuss each of the first seven
    novels.

2   MARIN, DANIEL B. "Voice and Structure in Saul Bellow's
    Novels." Ph.D. dissertation, University of Iowa, 275 pp.
    Listed in <u>Dissertation Abstracts International</u>, 33
    (12: June), 6920A-21A (Order No. 73,573).
        Bellow's verbal virtuosity creates a problem when his
    heroes' affirmations appear to be Bellow's and not their
    own. Bellow's major aesthetic problem "has been to develop
    a form that will give his affirmations the illusion of ob-
    jective impact and necessity." He has achieved this in
    <u>Henderson the Rain King</u>, <u>Herzog</u>, and <u>Mr. Sammler's Planet</u>.

3   WILLIAMS, PATRICIA W. "Saul Bellow's Fiction: A Critical
    Question." Ph.D. dissertation, Texas A & M University,
    264 pp. Listed in <u>Dissertation Abstracts International</u>,
    33 (May), 6379A-80A (Order No. 73-13,573).
        This study deals with the failure of the women in
    Bellow's novels to support his expressed philosophy. The
    female characters--the mothers, wives, ex-wives, and mis-
    tresses--are not presented as human beings; they assert the
    love so necessary to the realization of Bellow's world, but
    their love is not supported by the facts of the novels.

1973 B SHORTER WRITINGS

1   ALEXANDER, EDWARD. "Imagining the Holocaust: <u>Mr. Sammler's</u>
    <u>Planet</u> and Others." <u>Judaism</u>, 22 (Summer), 288-300.
       Sammler refuses to accept the idea that the evil of the
    mass murderers was banal. His own experiences suggest
    otherwise. He is subjected to irrationality and barbarism
    today as he was during the holocaust, but his experience of
    the death camps means that "he has already inhabited a dif-
    ferent world." This experience, "the ultimate reality of
    twentieth century life," is now the chief determinant of
    such life as is left to him. Bellow's "profoundly imagined
    re-creation" of this experience has its own authority.

2   ANON. Review article. <u>Nation</u>, 227 (17 December), 663.
       A brief article comparing Vonnegut's <u>Slaughterhouse Five</u>
    and <u>Mr. Sammler's Planet</u>.

3   AZANCOT, LEOPOLDO. "Saul Bellow, novelista de la modernidad."
    <u>Estafeta Literaria</u>, No. 510 (15 February), p. 1233.
       Bellow's novels develop both horizontally, emphasizing
    temporality and historicity, and vertically, emphasizing
    the human condition as a focus for eternal truths.

4   BAILEY, JENNIFER M. "The Qualified Affirmation of Saul
    Bellow's Recent Work." <u>Journal of American Studies</u>, 7
    (April), 67-76.
       In <u>Herzog</u> there is "a strong thread of ambiguous irony"
    which has deepened in <u>Mr. Sammler's Planet</u> into "uninten-
    tional parody." This shows Bellow's "inability to balance
    his protagonists' subjective reality with a convincing ver-
    sion of their social milieu." In this regard "Mosby's
    Memoirs" is somewhat more successful in that Bellow is able
    to achieve an imaginative connection with the world outside
    the self. His future success "depends upon an ability to
    incorporate an imaginative as well as intellectual energy
    in his writing."

5   BELL, PEARL K. "American Fiction: Forgetting the Ordinary
    Truths." <u>Dissent</u>, 20 (Winter), 26-34.
       In a discussion of recent American fiction, Bell finds
    <u>Mr. Sammler's Planet</u> one of the "few contemporary books
    that engage the mind and heart as one reads." Bellow
    brings an intellectual toughness to his portraits, and in
    Mr. Sammler one also senses his deep compassion.

6   BOYERS, ROBERT. "Nature and Social Reality in Bellow's
    <u>Sammler</u>." <u>Critical Quarterly</u>, 15 (Autumn), 251-71.

1973

        Examines the idea of nature in Bellow's writing (espe-
cially <u>Mr. Sammler's Planet</u>), and the relation of this idea
to two other ideas: the idea of social reality, and the
idea of character. There is an inconsistency in Bellow's
treatment of nature; it is difficult for us to understand
what Sammler desires for the world, and how he explains to
himself the idea of society and its relation to nature.
Bellow does not provide us with an understanding of the
forces which led up to the present moment in the novel.
In the universe Bellow gives us, "...the very idea of
nature has been altered, confused, deliberately turned
around in such a way that it does not mean what it used
to." And with the idea of nature perverted, it is also
difficult to think of social reality in customary ways.
This is Sammler's dilemma; nonetheless, we continue to
sympathize with him for he is decent, interesting, has
suffered, and is old.

7   BROMWICH, DAVID. "Some American Masks." <u>Dissent</u>, 20 (Winter),
     35-45.
        A consideration of the development of several artists
(particularly Bellow and Mailer) whose achievements seem
to be lasting. <u>The Adventures of Augie March</u> is close to
being a great novel. Augie is among Bellow's most disarming
masks; he is a discoverer who carefully steers "between the
highest seriousness and the lowest put-on." Augie is "Uni-
tarian at heart" because he always accepts, and seldom
shouts "No!" in thunder.

*8   BUITENHUIS, PETER. "A Corresponding Fabric: The Urban World
     of Saul Bellow." <u>Costerus</u>, 8 (1973), 13-36.
        Cited in <u>Modern Language Association International</u>
     <u>Bibliography</u>, 1 (1973), 155.

9   DICKSTEIN, FELICE W. "The Role of the City in the Works of
     Theodore Dreiser, Thomas Wolfe, James T. Farrell, and Saul
     Bellow." Ph.D. dissertation, City University of New York,
     191 pp. Listed in <u>Dissertation Abstracts International</u>,
     33 (11: May), 6350A (Order No. 73-11351).
        The city's presence is always felt in Bellow's novels,
and man's relation to it is a pervasive motif. Bellow
brilliantly dramatizes "the psychological consequences
arising out of the conditions of an urban life style."

10   EDWARDS, DUANE. "The Quest for Reality in <u>Henderson the Rain</u>
     <u>King</u>." <u>Dalhousie Review</u>, 53 (Summer), 246-55.
        Henderson's quest can be seen as his effort to create
and to replenish his own personal reality. In order to

catch glimpses of reality he is required to exert great
energy, effort, will, and discipline. He learns that
reality consists both of facts and illusions; accepting the
material world is vital, but he must also accept the reality of the mind that comes from within. He can cherish and
maintain his own illusions, if he does not move too far
outside of the "human theater."

*11 EROR, GVOZDEN. "Košmarna farsa o žrtvi Sola Beloua."
     Knijizevnost (Belgrade), 57 (1973), 99-108.
     Cited in Modern Language Association International
     Bibliography, 1 (1973), 155.

12 GALLOWAY, DAVID. "Mr. Sammler's Planet: Bellow's Failure of
    Nerve." Modern Fiction Studies, 19 (1973), 17-28.
        In Mr. Sammler's Planet Bellow continues to reflect his
    concern for the dilemma of modern man and the meaningless-
    ness of contemporary life. But the novel, while showing
    touches of genius "ultimately shows the bankruptcy of
    Bellow's novelistic imagination." Bellow's typical man-
    nerisms are intrusive in this novel because they are so
    obvious, and the work reveals a "fundamental disparity
    between action and idea or between image and symbol."

13 GUTTMANN, ALLEN. "Saul Bellow's Mr. Sammler." Contemporary
    Literature, 14 (Spring), 157-68.
        Many critics of Mr. Sammler's Planet, especially those
    associated with the "New Left," have complained that there
    is little or no ironic distance between Bellow and Sammler.
    This study attempts to show that there is considerable dif-
    ference between the two: their biographies, attitudes, and
    ideas are very different. Sammler's ideas are much more
    complex than have been acknowledged by such critics; and
    his humanism is both attractive and deeply moving.

14 KAZIN, ALFRED. Bright Book of Life: American Novelists and
    Storytellers from Hemingway to Mailer. Boston: Little,
    Brown and Co., pp. 125-38.
        The general theme of this book is the disintegration
    of the American social order after World War II; in pur-
    suing this theme Kazin compares the American Jewish expe-
    rience of Bellow, Malamud, and Roth. Chapter 5 provides
    an analysis of the impact on Bellow of such concepts as
    the embattled self, the Absurd, despair, and irrationality.
    Bellow, more than any other novelist of his ability, has
    used the modern Jewish experience in his work, but in so
    doing he has also conveyed "mass experience" to which any
    American can relate.

1973

15   KUGELMASS, HAROLD. "The Search for Identity: The Development
      of the Protean Model of Self in Contemporary American
      Fiction." Ph.D. dissertation, University of Oregon, 224 pp.
      Listed in Dissertation Abstracts International, 34
      (September), 1285A-86A (Order No. 73-20,218).
          Dangling Man is one of three modern novels studied which
      scrutinize the traditional model of self; such a model no
      longer provides a viable basis for establishing one's per-
      sonal identity. "Dangling Man demonstrates how man can use
      his consciousness to maintain a belief in an essential self
      and an identification of that self with reason which his
      actual situation invalidates."

16   LEWIS, STUART. "The Jewish Author Looks at the Black."
      Colorado Quarterly, 21 (Winter), 317-36.
          In supporting the thesis that the fiction of the American
      Jew reflects the Jew's ambivalence toward the black man,
      this essay considers selected fiction of Bellow, Leslie
      Fiedler, Bruce Jay Friedman, Gerald Green, Herbert Gold,
      Bernard Malamud, Philip Roth, Herbert Tarr, and Edward Lewis
      Wallant. There is a brief paragraph reference to
      Mr. Sammler's Planet with regard to the "Jew's fascination
      with the Black man's sexuality."

17   MALONEY, STEPHEN R. "Half-way to Byzantium: Mr. Sammler's
      Planet and the Modern Tradition." South Carolina Review,
      6 (i), 31-40.
          Bellow's development as a novelist can be compared with
      the movement of the persona in Yeat's "Sailing to Byzantium":
      from a passionate life and commitment to the flesh to an
      ascetic detachment as one finds in Sammler. Like Yeats'
      persona, Sammler wants to escape "from the bondage of the
      ordinary and finite," and to perceive "the greatness of
      eternity." In this novel Bellow clearly rejects sensual-
      ism, irrationality, and political radicalism, aligning him-
      self, instead, with the modernist movement of modern
      literature, and asserting religious values upon which his
      humanism and rationalism must rest.

18   MANSKE, EVA. "Das Menschenbild im Prosaschaffen Saul Bellows
      Anspruch und Wirklichkeit." Zeitschrift für Anglistik und
      Amerikanistik, 21 (1973), 270-88, 360-83.
          A novel by novel analysis, in German, through
      Mr. Sammler's Planet.

*19   MORO, KOCHI. "Monolog and Dialog: The Distance Between James
      Joyce and Saul Bellow." Josai Jinbun Kenkyu: Studies in
      the Humanities. Sakado, Iruma-Gun, Saitama, Japan: Josai
      University, Keizai-Gaku-Kai, pp. 102-31.

1973

Cited in <u>Modern Language Association International Bibliography</u>, 1 (1973), 155.

20 NADEL, MAX. <u>American Jewish Literature for High School Grades</u>. New York: Board of Jewish Education and New York Federation of Reform Synagogues.
Study questions and lesson guides for the teaching of <u>The Adventures of Augie March</u> (pp. 23-25) and <u>The Victim</u> (pp. 139-45).

21 PINSKER, SANFORD. "Saul Bellow in the Classroom." <u>College English</u>, 34 (April), 975-82.
This is a discussion between Bellow and a contemporary novel class at Franklin and Marshall College on May 22, 1972. Bellow answers questions on the relationship between a writer and the world of ideas, on Romanticism and its impact on contemporary culture, on <u>Herzog</u> and <u>Mr. Sammler's Planet</u>, on the source of Moses Herzog's name, on the influence of mass media, and on the religious response to the conditions of life.

22 RICHMOND, LEE J. "The Maladroit, the Medico, and the Magician: Saul Bellow's <u>Seize the Day</u>." <u>Twentieth Century Literature</u>, 19 (1973), 15-26.
The importance of Dr. Tamkin has been neglected in the criticism of <u>Seize the Day</u>. While Tamkin is a quack and a soldier of fortune, he is also a dealer in "magic" with power to heal diseased spirits. The ambiguity of his character allows for splendid detail and provides a key to the meaning of the novel.

*23 RODRIGUES, EUSEBIO L. "Bellow's Confidence Man." <u>Notes on Contemporary Literature</u>, 3 (i), 6-8.
Cited in <u>Modern Language Association International Bibliography</u>, 1 (1973), 155.

24 _____. "Reichianism in <u>Henderson the Rain King</u>. <u>Criticism</u>, 15 (Summer), 212-33.
<u>Henderson the Rain King</u> reveals Bellow's fascination with and creative use of the ideas and methods of Wilhelm Reich. Reich postulates a theory of the existence of an energy that "permeates all of nature and is a vital force in every human being." Man thwarts the free flow of this energy by his character armor and typical character attitudes. Henderson is an armored individual, and in going to Africa he seeks complete therapeutic transformation. In the novel there are three stages in the process of this transformation. In the last stage, the Reichian King Dhafu,

1973

helps to cure and educate Henderson, leading him to a
vision of the truth.

*25   ROSU, ANCA.   "The Picaresque Technique in Saul Bellow's
      Adventures of Augie March."   Analele Universitatii
      Bucuresti, Limbi Germanice, 22 (1973), 191-97.
          Cited in Modern Language Association International
      Bibliography, 1 (1973), 155.

*26   ROTHERMEL, WOLFGANG P.   "Saul Bellow," in Amerikanische
      Literatur der Gegenwart.   Edited by Martin Christadler.
      Stuttgart: Alfred Kroner, pp. 69-104.
          Cited in Modern Language Association International
      Bibliography, 1 (1973), 155.

27   RUSSELL, MARIANN.   "White Man's Black Man: Three Views."
      College Language Association Journal (Morgan State College,
      Baltimore), 17 (September), 93-100.
          Examines the roles played by Northern urban blacks
      appearing in three recent novels (Bellow's Mr. Sammler's
      Planet, John Updike's Rabbit Redux and Bernard Malamud's
      The Tenants) in order to see what the white authors have
      made of their black characters.   In Mr. Sammler's Planet
      Bellow portrays the black as primitive: a mad barbarian,
      a criminal, and sexually aggressive.   "He becomes an anal-
      ogy for those 'dark' forces of limitlessness, lawlessness,
      madness, and chaos that threaten to overcome the discipline
      and civility to which Sammler pays hard won tribute."
      Although Sammler is fascinated by him, he still remains a
      threatening, alien "other."

28   SCHULZ, MAX F.   "Mr. Bellow's Perigree, or, the Lowered Horizon
      of Mr. Sammler's Planet," in Contemporary American Jewish
      Literature.   Edited by Irving Malin.   Bloomington: Indiana
      University Press, pp. 117-33.
          Mr. Sammler's Planet represents a change of attitude in
      Bellow; it reflects "Bellow in retreat, turned off by the
      spectacle of a great city in disintegration and in recoil
      from a people bewildered by a 'new leisure and liberty.'"
      The change is reflected in Bellow's treatment of the novel's
      characters--disrespectful, contemptuous.   Bellow intellec-
      tualizes too much as Sammler seriously propounds his theo-
      ries.   Only Bellow's future writings will confirm whether
      this change is permanent.

29   SCOTT, NATHAN A., JR.   "Bellow's Vision of the 'Axial Lines,'"
      in Three American Novelists: Mailer, Bellow, Trilling.
      Notre Dame, Ind.:   University of Notre Dame Press, pp. 101-49.
          Revision of 1968.B20.

128

30 SHERES, ITA G. "Prophetic and Mystical Manifestations of Exile and Redemption in the Novels of Henry Roth, Bernard Malamud, and Saul Bellow." Ph.D. dissertation, University of Wisconsin, 330 pp. Listed in Dissertation Abstracts International, 33 (May), 6375A (Order No. 73-12117).
   The novels of these authors follow a pattern of alienation and illumination; or Exile and Redemption. Bellow's protagonists pursue a mystical pattern in an attempt to conquer Exile and be redeemed. "...it is easier to understand Bellow's writings if one sees them in the perspective of the 'Golem mysticism' which focuses on the more intellectual level of Redemption."

31 STEIG, MICHAEL. "Bellow's Henderson and the Limits of Freudian Criticism." Paunch (Buffalo), 36-37 (1973), 39-46.
   While Bellow uses Reichian concepts in Henderson the Rain King, one must consider some of his applications as a sympathetic parody, such as the Reichian therapeutic sessions with King Dahfu. Many passages in the novel reflect Reichian views of the relation between life-energy in humans and in the universe. A Freudian approach to the novel could have no claim of applicability in interpreting Bellow's work.

*32 STEINKE, RUSSELL. "The Monologic Temper of Bellow's Fiction." Junction (Brooklyn College), 1 (iii), 178-84.
   Cited in Modern Language Association International Bibliography, 1 (1973), 155.

33 TIJERAS, EDUARDO. "Saul Bellow." Cuadernos Hispanoamericanos (Madrid), 274 (1973), 182-86.
   A brief article, in Spanish, dealing primarily with Herzog and Mr. Sammler's Planet. Bellow is considered to be one of the finest of North American novelists.

34 WEINSTEIN, NORMAN. "Herzog, Order and Entropy." English Studies, 54 (1973), 336-46.
   Herzog, like Ulysses, is an attempt to create some order and unity in a world of chaos and despair. The book represents Herzog's "search for order using his own point of departure, the law of entropy, as a model." Herzog has an acute unrelatedness within himself, to the rest of mankind, and to the physical universe. To gain order he must discover relationships; he must bind together his dynamic notions of physical, biological and social order into a grand synthesis. In his attempts to discover order, Herzog displays a firmer grasp of those aspects of modern science and technology which directly affect the mind and experience than most humanists and intellectuals today.

1973

35 ZEITLOW, E. R. "Saul Bellow: The Theater of the Soul."
    Ariel: A Review of International English Literature, 4
    (October), 44-59.
        In Henderson the Rain King, Herzog, and Mr. Sammler's
    Planet, Bellow develops a vision of the conduct of life as
    a "theater of the soul." Specific actions in this theater
    function to further or retard the growth of that soul.
    Bellow's emphasis on the soul contrasts with the pessimis-
    tic existentialism of many contemporary writers. In creat-
    ing a post-Modern hero in Sammler, Bellow restores spiritual
    depth to the self, but this depth is created by an internal
    rather than an external authority.

1974 A BOOKS

1   COHEN, SARAH BLACHER. Saul Bellow's Enigmatic Laughter.
    Urbana, Ill.: University of Illinois Press, 242 pp.
        A revision of a dissertation, 1970.A1. In this study
    of Bellow's comedy, Cohen shows how Bellow, when tempted
    to despair, retaliates with comedy. A chapter is devoted
    to the comedy in each of the novels. In Dangling Man and
    The Victim comedy "acts as a shaky defense which ineffec-
    tually staves off distrust and melancholy." In The Adven-
    tures of Augie March comedy serves "as a miraculous
    alchemizer which transforms the common into the precious."
    In Seize the Day comedy is a shield employed by Bellow "to
    protect him against his ubiquitous harassers." In Henderson
    the Rain King comedy is used to defend and undercut
    Henderson's "vaunted image of himself and to attack his
    brute opponents." In Herzog comedy acts as a balance and
    a barricade "to counter and combat his own depressive ten-
    dencies and the apocalyptic pronouncements of the reigning
    cognoscenti." In Mr. Sammler's Planet comedy serves as "a
    confectionary to accompany the bitter views of an old man."
    Bellow becomes progressively more sophisticated and versa-
    tile in his use of the comic mode; and such comedy brings
    us "relief from the long prevalent mood of pessimism, dis-
    couragement, and low-seriousness."
        A bibliography of sources cited is included, pp. 224-30.

2   MORAHAG, GILEAD. "Idea as a Thematic Element in Saul Bellow's
    'Victim' Novels." Ph.D. dissertation, University of Wis-
    consin, 226 pp. Listed in Dissertation Abstracts Inter-
    national, 34 (10: April), 6599A (Order No. 73-32,134).
        A study of ideas as a thematic element in Dangling Man,
    The Victim, and Seize the Day. The transformation of the
    protagonists in these novels is primarily intellectual;

WRITINGS ABOUT SAUL BELLOW, 1944-1976

their intellectual growth is imperative before they are
delivered from victimization, since they are victimized by
their philosophical disorientation to social circumstances.
Bellow's vision of man's attempt to overcome victimization
is given literary life through his effective dramatization
of action and ideas.

3   PORTER, M. GILBERT. Whence the Power? The Artistry and Human-
    ity of Saul Bellow. Columbia, Missouri: University of
    Missouri Press, 209 pp.
       In this study a chapter is devoted to each of the novels
    with a concluding chapter on Bellow's vision. Using a "for-
    malist" critical stance with close analysis of intrarefer-
    ential relations, Porter first examines the identity crisis
    of Joseph, then the issue of guilt and responsibility in
    The Victim, the play of opposites in The Adventures of
    Augie March, the image of man drowning in Seize the Day,
    physical and spiritual regeneration in Henderson the Rain
    King, the chaos of personal life in Herzog, and the uneasy
    relation between themes and fictional concretions in
    Mr. Sammler's Planet. Finally, Bellow's creative vision
    is considered as a part of a "neo-transcendentalism" liter-
    ary tradition.
       A bibliography is included, pp. 199-209.

1974 B SHORTER WRITINGS

1   BOLLING, DOUGLASS. "Intellectual and Aesthetic Dimensions of
    Mr. Sammler's Planet." Journal of Narrative Technique, 4
    (September), 188-203.
       An argument for the excellence of Mr. Sammler's Planet
    through a discussion of the novel's controlling aesthetic
    and intellectual background. The novel is based on "the
    principle of contrast and opposition rather than that of a
    dialectical tension leading to a synthesizing conclusion."
    Two major patterns of the novel generate its substance and
    maintain its tension. One pattern is meditative: it in-
    volves Sammler's philosophical concerns which are presented
    at a speculative and intellectual level. The other pattern
    involves the dominant action of the novel: the effort to
    recover Lal's manuscript. The six major chapters of the
    novel are "shaped so as to forward and enhance thematic
    and fictive rhythms."

*2 BROPHY, ROBERT J. "Biblical Parallels in Bellow's Henderson
    the Rain King." Christianity and Literature, 23 (iv),
    27-30.
       Cited in Modern Language Association International
    Bibliography, 1 (1974), 168.

Writings about Saul Bellow, 1944-1976

*3 COHEN, SARAH B. "Sex: Saul Bellow's Hedonistic Joke."
    Studies in American Fiction, 2 (1974), 223-29.
    Cited in Modern Language Association International
    Bibliography, 1 (1974), 168.

4   FUCHS, DANIEL. "Saul Bellow and the Modern Tradition."
    Contemporary Literature, 15 (Winter), 67-89.
    Bellow is a post-modern writer who rejects the modernist
    position which originated in nineteenth-century French lit-
    erature. His central thrust is "to deny nihilism, immoral-
    ism, and the aesthetic view." A review of his novels
    clearly shows how the aesthetic gives way to the ethical,
    and the artist to the thinker. Mr. Sammler's Planet is
    bleaker than the earlier novels, for Sammler experiences
    a society in which modernism has triumphed.

5   GUERARD, ALBERT J. "Saul Bellow und die Aktivisten: Über
    The Adventures of Augie March," in Der amerikanische Roman
    im 19. und 20. Jahrhundert. Edited by Edgar Lohner.
    Berlin: Erich Schmidt, pp. 353-65.
    A translation into German of 1967.B13.

6   HULLY, KATHLEEN. "Disintegration as Symbol of Community: A
    Study of The Rainbow, Women in Love, Light in August, Pris-
    oner of Grace, Except the Lord, Not Honour More, and Herzog."
    Ph.D. dissertation, University of California, Davis,
    307 pp. Listed in Dissertation Abstracts International,
    34:6643A-44A (Order No. 74-8513.
    The novels, including Herzog, are examined in terms of
    their negative structures and negative characterizations:
    the characters recoil from connection with others, are pas-
    sive, and feel ashamed, ironic, and guilty for their retreat.

7   HUX, SAMUEL. "Character and Form in Bellow." Forum (Univer-
    sity of Houston), 12 (Spring), 34-38.
    One should not be condescending toward the expansiveness
    and apparent looseness of style and wit in Bellow, nor of
    the apparent looseness in structure; these are his strengths.
    "...the use and direction of Bellow's fiction requires a
    particular kind of form, and his apparent looseness is pre-
    cisely that form." Bellow's characters are always in the
    process of change, even at the end of the novels, and thus
    the endings must remain "open."

8   JEFCHAK, ANDREW. "Family Struggles in Seize the Day." Studies
    in Short Fiction, 11 (Summer), 297-302.
    Family relationships tend to dictate all of the actions
    in Seize the Day. Of greatest importance is the father/son

relationship between Dr. Adler and Tommy, and the husband/
wife relationship between Tommy and Margaret. In the
father/son relationship none of the typical concern, sympathy, and respect exist. In the husband/wife relationship,
Margaret offers tension and anguish instead of love, understanding, and support.

9   LAMONT, ROSETTE C. "Bellow Observed: A Serial Portrait."
Mosaic: A Journal for the Comparative Study of Literature
and Ideas, 8 (Fall), 247-57.
A significant portrait of Bellow, detailing selected
incidents in his life since 1960. Bellow's interest, attitudes, and life style are delineated, supported by quota-
tions and quips from conversations.

10   MELLARD, JAMES. "Dangling Man: Saul Bellow's Lyrical Expe-
riment." Ball State University Forum, 15 (Spring), 67-74.
Earlier criticism has not confronted the serious formal
experimentation in which Bellow was obviously engaged in
writing Dangling Man. The novel is best understood as a
piece of lyrical fiction where action in time and space are
not vitally significant, where the shape of the novel is
determined by the protagonist's point of view, and where
the reader must "be even more attuned to unexpected asso-
ciative connections than the protagonist."

11   RODRIGUES, EUSEBIO L. "Koheleth in Chicago: The Quest for
the Real in 'Looking for Mr. Green.'" Studies in Short
Fiction, 11 (Fall), 387-93.
This story is a minor classic of our time, perhaps
Bellow's most complete and compact short story. By carefully analyzing the story we can see how Bellow transforms
a Dreiserian tale into a metaphysical parable. In hunting
for Mr. Green, Grebe, a modern Koheleth, is also searching
for the meaning of human existence.

12   SUSMAN, MAXINE S. "Interpretation of Jewish Character in
Renaissance and Recent Literature." Ph.D. dissertation,
Cornell University, 288 pp. Listed in Dissertation
Abstracts International, 35: 1063A.
In Mr. Sammler's Planet, the stereotype of the old,
alien, lonely Jew is transformed through Sammler's rein-
terpretation of the Jewish ideal of the moral covenant,
i.e., fulfilling the terms of his human contract.

1975

1   LEESE, DAVID ALLEN. "Laughter in the Ghetto: A Study of
     Form in Saul Bellow's Comedy." Ph.D. dissertation,
     Brandeis University, 168 pp. Listed in <u>Dissertation
     Abstracts International</u>, 36 (1: July), 321A (Order No.
     75-15,112).
          Includes three theoretical studies of Bellow's comedy
     (the enigmatic endings from the perspective of classical
     comic theory; the relation of Bellow's comic style to his
     rejection of the Absurd; and the relation of Bellow's
     intellectual pursuits and his comedy); and three detailed
     examinations of form (<u>Dangling Man</u>, "Leaving the Yellow
     House," and <u>Seize the Day</u>).

2   MARCUS, DIANA. "The Rehumanization of Art: Secondary Charac-
     terizations in the Novels of Saul Bellow." Ph.D. disserta-
     tion, Wayne State University, 477 pp. Listed in
     <u>Dissertation Abstracts International</u>, 35 (12: June),
     7903A (Order No. 75-13,312).
          Bellow's secondary characters are examined in each of
     the novels in terms of whether they are primarily <u>dramatic</u>
     and involved in the central action of the novel, or whether
     they are primarily <u>social</u> and not involved in central
     action. Whether clowns or fools, victims or predators,
     romantics or realists, these secondary characters "invest
     the novels with a magnetic affirmation of life toward which
     most modern readers are irresistibly drawn."

3   RIEHL, BETTY ANN JONES. "Narrative Structure in Saul Bellow's
     Novels." Ph.D. dissertation University of Texas, Austin,
     153 pp. Listed in <u>Dissertation Abstracts International</u>, 36
     (5: November), 2827A (Order No. 24,945).
          A narrative analysis of the structures of Bellow's novels
     reveals a decreasing distance between author and protagonist
     over the course of the seven novels.

4   ROVIT, EARL, ed. <u>Saul Bellow: A Collection of Critical
     Essays</u>. Englewood Cliffs: Prentice-Hall, 176 pp.
          This collection includes essays or parts of larger
     works that treat as full a sampling of Bellow's production
     as possible. Included are "Saul Bellow: An Interview" by
     Gordon Harper (1966.B24); "<u>Dangling Man</u>" by Denis Donoghue
     (1968.B2); "<u>The Victim</u>" by John Clayton (1968.A1); "Scene
     as Image: <u>Seize the Day</u>" by M. Gilbert Porter (1975.B28);
     "Ambiguous Assault of Henderson and Herzog" by Richard
     Pearce (1975.B26); "<u>Herzog</u>, or Bellow in Trouble" by
     Richard Poirer (1965.B44); "The Schlemiel as Liberal

Humanist" by Ruth Wisse (1975.B42); "Battle of the Sexes in Three Bellow Novels" by Victoria Sullivan (1975.B38); "Bummy's Analysis" by Irving Malin (1975.B21); "Bellow and Mr. Sammler" by Ben Siegel (1975.B36); "Discipline of Nobility: Bellow's Fiction" by Marcus Klein (1962.B4); "Bellow and Mailer: The Secret Sharers" by Earl Rovit (1975.B31).

The essays by Malin, Pearce, Porter, Siegel, Sullivan, and Rovit appear for the first time in this collection. A chronology of Bellow and a bibliography are also included.

5   SCHULWEIS, MALKAH. "The Concept of the Self in Saul Bellow's Novels." M.A. thesis, California State University, Northridge.

After considering the radical change in the view of the self which developed in the nineteenth century, making the self the sole source of cognition, value and meaning, Schulweis traces the development of the self in The Adventures of Augie March, Seize the Day, Henderson the Rain King, and Herzog.

6   SEWELL, WILLIAM JACOB. "Literary Structure and Value Judgment in the Novels of Saul Bellow." Ph.D. dissertation, Duke University, 278 pp. Listed in Dissertation Abstracts International, 35 (9: March), 6159A (Order No. 75-6784).

An examination of Bellow's use of narrative formal devices to provide literary structures through which he dramatizes his value judgments. These judgments focus upon man's need for individuality "through an alienation-reconciliation pattern. The pattern consists of temporary separation from social conformity as a means towards a private reconciliation with society and therein reconciliation with the self."

7   WALLACH, JUDITH DANA LOWENTHAL. "The Quest for Selfhood in Saul Bellow's Novels: A Jungian Interpretation." Ph.D. dissertation, University of Victoria, Canada. Listed in Dissertation Abstracts International, 36 (5: November), 2829A.

This study utilizes the insights of Jungian psychology, "with its understanding of the archetypes of the collective unconscious and its explication of the process of individuation, to analyze the psychological conflicts of Bellow's protagonists and to reveal the underlying unity and progression within his fiction." His novels represent the collective journey of contemporary man toward the realization of soul.

1975

1975 B SHORTER WRITINGS

1   AARON, DANIEL. Review of Humboldt's Gift. New Republic, 173
    (20 September), 28.
        "Marginal Notes" are provided for Humboldt's Gift, in-
    cluding comment on the ideal reader for the book, Bellow's
    favorite themes, characterizations of Charlie Citrine and
    Humboldt, Charlie's solution to the death question, and
    boredom. Bellow has a "turned-on mind," a talent for
    absurdity and wit, and gift for entertaining.

2   ALDRIDGE, JOHN. "Saul Bellow at 60: A Turn to the Mystical."
    Saturday Review, 2 (6 September), 22-25.
        Citrine is one of Bellow's most convincing characters--
    his life is that of "a relentlessly secular existence." In
    Humboldt's Gift Bellow has been "able to objectify his own
    wishful optimism and to accept it for just that, declining
    to give it a more crucial thematic importance." The novel
    does not display a synthesis of its metaphysical and secu-
    lar material; but its power comes from "the quality and
    intensity of the felt life contained within it, the bril-
    liant evocation of the social world, and the incredible
    sensitivity of its characterizations."

3   ALLEN, BRUCE. Review of Humboldt's Gift. Library Journal,
    100 (1 November), 2067.
        Brief notice: Bellow "has plotted this book generously,
    and studded it with a calculated ebullience that engages
    and charms." The book reveals the unmistakable markings
    of "compassionate maturity."

4   ANON. Review of Humboldt's Gift. Choice, 12 (November), 1159.
        A major novel "of impressive proportions" which wrestles
    with the greatest of issues, Humboldt's Gift concerns a
    suffering hero at the last rites of the twentieth century.

5   AXELROD, STEVEN G. "The Jewishness of Bellow's Henderson."
    American Literature, 47 (November), 439-43.
        Although Henderson is intended as the archetypal gentile
    American, he is implicitly Jewish: in appearance, he con-
    forms to the Jewish stereotype, he defines himself in Jew-
    ish terms, he is an outcast and a schlemiel, and he
    transforms himself into Daniel, the survivor of lion's dens.
    In Henderson, Bellow "discovers the Jewish within an
    American Everyman."

6   BELL, PEARL. "Bellow's Best and Worst." New Leader, 58
    (1 September), 19-20.

Humboldt's Gift is both Bellow's best and least satisfying novel. The brilliance of characterization and exuberance of ideas are there, but when Charlie opens Humboldt's
letter from the grave, the novel falls apart with implausi-
bility. The major problem is that no one in the novel con-
veys Bellow's own moral and intellectual opinions; he is
"curiously detached."

7 BRADBURY, MALCOLM. "The It and the We." Encounter, 45
   (November), 61-67.
       In Humboldt's Gift, Bellow has "bounced back, back to
   the panoramic, picaresque, ebullient vein of some of his
   earlier novels...and to his resilient registering of the
   contemporary consciousness." Absurdity in his novels
   leads to a modified realism; Bellow always attempts to
   reconcile the mind with the burdensome body. He does so
   in Humboldt's Gift, for it basically is "an attempt at a
   culture-reading of an American split between overwhelming
   mass and material substance and the desire for mind, between the It and the We...." The characters are essentially portraits of historical consciousness, and although
   the novel flags at the end, it is throughout invested with
   Bellow's deep comedy and insights, a "testament to his
   range and versatility."

8 BROYARD, ANATOLE. "Lion or the Anthroposophist?" New York
   Times, 124 (14 August), 29.
       Humboldt's Gift is a disappointing novel; it reflects a
   distrust of ideas, Bellow's thoughts are not integrated with
   the action, the "gift" is anticlimactic, and the protagonist
   is dull, without significant relationships.

9 CLEMONS, WALTER, and JACK KROLL. "America's Master Novelist."
   Newsweek, 86 (1 September), 32-34, 39-40.
       Bellow's career has been remarkable, and Humboldt's Gift
   consolidates his position as America's greatest contemporary
   writer, and one of the all time great masters of narrative
   voice and perspective. The novel reflects Bellow's renewed,
   serious interest in the life of the spirit; it also shows
   that his gifts as a writer have not failed, but, rather,
   matured. Bellow's life in Chicago is reported on; Bellow
   comments on the writing of Humboldt's Gift, Rudolf Steiner's
   philosophy, political involvement, and his own future as a
   writer.

10 COOK, BRUCE. "Bellow Chooses Chicago, America, and Life."
    National Observer, 14 (30 August), 19.

1975

Humboldt's Gift may well be the best novel of Bellow's
career. It is a "nearly 500-page meditation on mortality
interrupted intermittently and hilariously with farcical
action." In it the values are topsy-turvy; "all the greed
in it is directed toward emblems of the spirit." Cook
reflects upon his impressions of Bellow when he interviewed
him in 1963 (See 1963.B3).

11   CUSHMAN, K. "Discriminating Gusto." Chicago Review, 27
      (Winter, 1975/76), 145-48.
      Humboldt's Gift is a series of brilliant episodes, with
      a frenetic, somewhat lengthy pace. At times it seems too
      self-indulgent, too autobiographical, but the gusto of
      Bellow's style redeems it. "Bellow seems to be suggesting
      that although we reach for transcendence, we are trapped in
      a world of shenanigans; let us learn to live in it."

12   DURHAM, JOYCE ROBERTA. "The City in Recent American Litera-
      ture: Black on White. A Study of Selected Writings of
      Bellow, Mailer, Ellison, Baldwin, and Writers of the Black
      Aesthetic." Ph.D. dissertation, University of Maryland,
      293 pp. Listed in Dissertation Abstracts International,
      36 (3: September), 1501A (Order No. 75-18,752).
      A study of how black values have historically been
      superimposed on the more dominant mores of white society.
      Bellow uses the city as a metaphor for a meaningless uni-
      verse. While effectively rendering physical environments,
      Bellow focuses upon intellectual estrangement from the city.

13   FULLER, EDMUND. "Cowing Before the 'Gorgeous Project.'" Wall
      Street Journal, 186 (27 August), 10.
      Humboldt's Gift is a bulky, overlong comedy, but Bellow
      does create some warmth and hope in the novel's ending.
      The characterization of Humboldt is one of Bellow's finest
      achievement.

14   GIANNONE, RICHARD. "Saul Bellow's Idea of Self: A Reading of
      Seize the Day." Renascence, 27 (Summer), 193-205.
      An examination of the form of Seize the Day to show how
      Bellow "brings the Romantic idea of self to a position of
      structural determination by making his central figure an
      inadvertant aspirant to a Romantic ambition." The novel is
      structured around Tommy Wilhelm's being successively
      "stripped of the more-than-human versions of himself in
      order to reach his humanness." To seize the day, he must
      shed the idea of himself that he has outworn.

15 GILMAN, RICHARD. Review of Humboldt's Gift. New York Times
    Book Review (17 August), p. 1.
        Bellow's writing is characterized by "its sense of moral
    and social crisis, its agitated ambivalence toward experi-
    ence, its furious humor and cry of mingled warning and en-
    lightenment." Humboldt's Gift is no exception to this,
    although it is a much more relaxed book, much more open and
    ingratiating than his earlier novels. The book is spacious
    and lengthy--but only because its theme requires a "slow
    accretion of recognitions, a painstaking working out of a
    plan of escape." The novel's overall action, however, is
    not as important nor satisfying as the significant ideas
    and intuitions that Bellow provides along the way.

16 GORNICK, VIVIAN. "Saul Bellow: Couch in the Mouth." Village
    Voice, 20 (18 August), 43.
        Humboldt's Gift neither illuminates nor transforms the
    woe of its protagonist, Citrine. Citrine is manic and
    hysterical; he is "a protagonist in the lifelong grip of
    mewling fantasy unblemished by even the faintest struggle
    to mature out of the cloying past." He talks nonstop but
    little happens to him that matters to us; all other char-
    acters in the book, particularly the women, are mere
    caricatures. The relationships are thin and vacuous, lack-
    ing in real emotional involvement. Unlike Joseph, Leventhal,
    and Tommy Wilhelm, Bellow's later characters do experience
    life or suffer pain and reluctant self-knowledge that is
    transmitted to the reader. The later characters are merely
    talking, outwitting their analyst.

17 KIRSCH, ROBERT. "Bellow Looks Beneath the Laughter." Los
    Angeles Times Book Review (24 August), pp. 1, 12.
        In Humboldt's Gift Bellow's treatment of the theme of
    the artist's role in the world is "daring and paradoxically
    fresh." The novel proceeds on two levels--the realistic,
    funny episodes which are vintage Bellow, and the search for
    a deeper significance in life. The artist, Humboldt, repre-
    sents a part of all of us who still believe in the mysteri-
    ous words, Beauty, Meaning, Love, Soul. The novel suggests
    that there is something beyond absurdity and the fashionable
    cynicism of our time. The novel is imposing, "an antidote
    to the depressing insistence of the common crisis as the
    inevitable fate of man, speaking hauntingly of redemption."

18 KLAUSLER, ALFRED. "Innocent Cunning." Christian Century,
    92 (24 September), 827-29.
        Humboldt's Gift reaffirms that the novel is alive and
    well; Bellow's comedy is in the Balzac traditon, his

1975

> laughter near tears. All of us share in the qualities of
> Citrine: his innocence alternates with devious cunning,
> his tenuous experiences reflect the fragility of life.

19 LEMON, L. T. "Bellow's Encore." Prairie Schooner, 49
    (Winter, 1975/76), 360-61.
    While Bellow's strength has always been in his ability
    to create believable intellectuals who know and feel a
    great deal, and who make their knowing a part of their
    lives, he fails in Humboldt's Gift to maintain his custom-
    ary strength: our expectations that Citrine and Humboldt
    will speak and act like brilliant intellectuals is not
    fulfilled.

20 LODGE, DAVID. "Dead Reckoning." Times Literary Supplement
    (10 October), p. 1173.
    A book about death and its metaphysical implications and
    money, Humboldt's Gift would have been improved with ruth-
    less cutting. The spiritual-metaphysical quest sags some-
    what in the middle, but the book is redeemed by its fine
    comic moments, its descriptions of Chicago, and its "bril-
    liant mimicry of lawyers, businessmen, and crooks."

21 MALIN, IRVING. "Bummy's Analysis," in Saul Bellow: A Collec-
    tion of Critical Essays. Edited by Earl Rovit. Englewood
    Cliffs, N. J.: Prentice-Hall, pp. 115-121.
    An "intensive," theoretical analysis of The Last Anal-
    ysis. Malin explores the mental comedy of the play, and
    finds its final effect to be mixed. Bummidge "lacks the
    'mental comedy' for higher elevation."

22 MANO, D. KEITH. "Bellow's Dead Center." National Review, 27
    (7 November), 1246.
    Though not his best novel, Humboldt's Gift could be
    Bellow's most significant book; it is "Bellow's most open,
    unreserved, personal book," more akin to confessional auto-
    biography than the typical novel. It is sometimes sloppy,
    with offhand, amicable prose, and Bellow's obsession with
    Chicago is obvious; here he has made of it a foreign enclave.
    But the haunting center of the book is what Citrine talks
    around, fears, and avoids: the possibility of Grace.

23 McEWAN, IAN. "An American Dream." Spectator, 235
    (11 October), 478.
    Although sprawling and somewhat clumsy in form,
    Humboldt's Gift reflects Bellow as a mature, deliberate
    artist. Bellow's cultural eclecticism help make it a rich,
    brave, and compelling book.

24 NEWMAN, CHARLES. "Lives of the Artists." Harper's Magazine,
     251 (October), 82-85.
          Charles Citrine is familiar, yet different from Bellow's
     other characters: in comparison to others, he might be
     clichéd and pretentious, morally passive and intellectually
     sloppy, yet his metaphysical and mystical bent has given
     him "a rare sense of the continuity between the dead and
     the living." The novel reaffirms Bellow's position as a
     realist, one who firmly believes in correspondence between
     inner and outer worlds.

25 NORDELL, RODERICK. "Humboldt's Gift Arrives." Christian
     Science Monitor (27 August), p. 23.
          While Humboldt's Gift does not have the kinetic language
     of Augie March, nor the inventiveness of Henderson, it does
     reflect Bellow's continued refusal to give up on humanity.

26 PEARCE, RICHARD. "The Ambiguous Assault of Henderson and
     Herzog," in Saul Bellow: A Collection of Critical Essays.
     Edited by Earl Rovit. Englewood Cliffs, N. J.: Prentice-
     Hall, pp. 72-80.
          Henderson assaults reality physically; Herzog assaults
     reality with language. In Henderson, Bellow has created
     "an ambiguous hero, sensitive and blustering, intelligent
     and buffoonish, reflective and impulsive, in touch intel-
     lectually with the main currents of modern life and pug-
     naciously anti-intellectual." The ambiguity of Herzog's
     assault "derives from an agon between consciousness and
     grammar--between reality as it is perceived phenomenolog-
     ically and the order required for making sentences."

27 PEARSON, GABRIEL. "Human Tissues." Guardian Weekly, 113
     (19 October), 24.
          Humboldt's Gift clearly indicates that the novel has
     collapsed as a significant form. There is nothing in the
     novel but the oppressive self-consciousness of Citrine.
     The novel reflects a typical American cannibalism: the
     "consumption of its own flesh and blood and brilliant
     energies."

28 PORTER, M. GILBERT. "The Scene as Image: A Reading of Seize
     the Day," in Saul Bellow: A Collection of Critical Essays.
     Edited by Earl Rovit. Englewood Cliffs, N. J.: Prentice-
     Hall, pp. 52-71.
          This essay appeared in slightly different form in
     Porter, 1974.A3
          An attempt to demonstrate the usefulness of applying a
     formalist critical methodology to a reading of Seize the

1975

Day. Taking the central metaphor of the novel, that of
depicting human failure through the image of a drowning
man, Porter examines in detail the eight scenes of the
novel, each of which functions as a dimension of the total
image.

29   PRITCHETT, V. S. "Potatoe Pie." New Statesman, 90
        (10 October), 442-43.
            In Humboldt's Gift, Bellow again shows himself a "master
        of elaborately patterned narrative that slips back or for-
        ward in time." Chicago is the hero of the novel; no other
        American novelist can match Bellow in portraying the urban
        scene. With tact and irony, Bellow makes the boring in-
        triguing. The one flaw of the novel is that Bellow spins
        himself into a web of dramatic situations two-thirds of the
        way through, and never fully extricates himself.

30   RICHARDSON, JACK. "A Burnt-Out Case." Commentary, 60
        (November), 74-78.
            In Humboldt's Gift Bellow's arena has become much
        smaller than in previous novels. This is a "sad, shallow
        book, a statement of intellectual and artistic surrender
        that has as its only interesting quality that crude sense
        of humor a writer can sometimes wring out of the willful
        abasement of his characters." Bellow fails to demonstrate
        convincingly Humboldt's significant qualities, and Citrine
        himself is a burnt-out case, only rescued in the end with
        "heavy handed irony."

31   ROVIT, EARL. "Saul Bellow and Norman Mailer: The Secret
        Sharers," in his Edition of Saul Bellow: A Collection of
        Critical Essays. Englewood, Cliffs, N. J.: Prentice-Hall,
        pp. 161-70.
            American fiction of the fifties and sixties has been
        heavily dominated by the collision of claims and counter-
        claims associated with the radically different styles of
        Bellow and Mailer. In spite of seeming incompatibility,
        both writers have been working along parallel lines. Both
        writers "found their early work on very similar legacies.
        Both inherit a defining naturalistic concept of world
        order, and both wage valiant battle against the paralyzing
        burden of that concept." Despite their distinctive tem-
        peramental differences, they have a "close mutuality of
        vision and technique."

32   RULE, PHILIP C. Review of Humboldt's Gift. America, 133
        (20 December), 445.

Humboldt's Gift lacks none of Bellow's intellectual
vigor and artistic range. Though basically optimistic in
his outlook, Bellow is nonetheless a realist; he may be
moving toward "Wordsworthian natural mysticism."

33   SALE, ROGER. "The Realms of Gold." Hudson Review, 28
     (Winter, 1975-76), 623-25.
         Although Humboldt's Gift echoes with the sounds of
     Bellow's earlier characters (especially all the reality
     instructors), it is as good, if not better, than his pre-
     vious novels. But the last one hundred pages "are a mess";
     even so, "it fails at a level no other American writer
     tries to reach."

34   SHATTUCK, ROGER. "A Higher Selfishness?" New York Review of
     Books, 22 (18 September), 21-25.
         In Humboldt's Gift, the solitude of Bellow's earlier
     books "is becoming very real and leans toward self-
     absorption." The book is marked with more irony and more
     intense philosophizing. It reveals Bellow's gift for
     creating an air of reality and then moving beyond it. He
     is able to digress and accumulate detail, while maintaining
     confidence in the story he is telling. The novel is per-
     haps flawed by a lack of economy in some scenes, and by its
     apparent autobiographical content and its near obsession
     with Rudolf Steiner's doctrines. The "fictional impulse
     is out of adjustment," even though the novel shows no
     decline in Bellow's intelligence and stylistic powers.

35   SHEPPARD, R. S. "Scribbler on the Roof." Time, 106
     (25 August), 62.
         In Humboldt's Gift, Bellow still provides us with old
     fashioned characters and a presentation of "big ideas as
     if they were messages from a philosophical sponsor." The
     novel would be morose and tedious were it not for Bellow's
     remarkable gifts as a storyteller and his talent for vivid
     characterization.

36   SIEGEL, BEN. "Saul Bellow and Mr. Sammler: Absurd Seekers
     of High Qualities," in Saul Bellow: A Collection of
     Critical Essays. Edited by Earl Rovit. Englewood Cliffs,
     N. J.: Prentice-Hall, pp. 122-34.
         In Mr. Sammler's Planet Bellow once again transmutes
     into fiction "those forces that isolate the sensitive
     American from his peers." Here Bellow sympathizes with
     the young radicals living in the turbulent sixties, but
     he scorns their behavior and their inability to attempt
     viable solutions. Through Sammler, Bellow voices his

1975

objection to mass obsession of negating culture, the past,
and civilized order. He decries the wasted human poten-
tial. Siegel responds to many of the critical attacks on
Bellow for the positions taken in the novel.

37 STERN, DANIEL. "The Bellow-ing of the Culture." Commonweal,
    102 (24 October), 502-04.
       Humboldt's Gift is "a magnificent, major work of the
    cultured imagination, stymied at the crossroads of life,
    death, and thought." It is Bellow's best novel, richly
    textured, and again confronting his enduring themes. The
    novel raises the question whether our ideas are really used
    up, or whether they are merely metamorphosizing into other
    ideas through which life can again become viable.

38 SULLIVAN, VICTORIA. "The Battle of the Sexes in Three Bellow
    Novels," in Saul Bellow: A Collection of Critical Essays.
    Edited by Earl Rovit. Englewood Cliffs, N. J.: Prentice-
    Hall, pp. 101-114.
       Bellow's women are either victims or victimizers—all
    of them strange, illogical, and disturbing. Analysis of
    the battle of the sexes in Herzog, Seize the Day, and
    Henderson the Rain King reveals that there are no winners
    in this battle, even though Bellow naturally aligns himself
    with the men. Relationships between the sexes cause pain
    and are spiritually debilitating; love seems doomed.
    Bellow is not sexist, but he is not very hopeful about
    satisfaction in male-female relationships.

39 TOYNBEE, PHILIP. "Matter of Life and Death." The Observer
    (5 October), p. 23.
       Humboldt's Gift is Bellow's best novel; it is the
    "nearest American approach to Dostoevsky's The Idiot and
    The Brother's Karamazov." In this novel Bellow "has trans-
    cended, though not neglected, the whole socio-political
    field, in favour of a tentative but fervent plea for a new
    look at the needs, and the present state of the human soul."
    The novel is both funny and deeply serious, and, surpris-
    ingly, Bellow pulls it off "with superb panache."

40 TURNER, THEODORE BAKER, III. "Mind Forged Manacles: Images
    of the University in American Fiction of the Nineteen
    Sixties. A Study in Kesey, Mailer, Barth, Bellow, Nabakov,
    and Burroughs." Ph.D. dissertation, The University of
    Iowa, 254 pp. Listed in Dissertation Abstracts Inter-
    national, 35 (7: January), 4566A (Order No. 75-1279).
       A study of the surprising interest in universities, uni-
    versity people, and the growth and training of the mind

reflected in these six prominent writers during the six-
ties. Bellow, like Barth and Nabakov, tends to have "an
air of self-mocking, satirical disgust toward the educa-
tional world...." Yet hope is placed in the universities
for here the verbal, ideal world, the political world, and
the world searching for a true consciousness exist side
by side.

41 UPDIKE, JOHN. "Draping Radiance with a Worn Veil." The New
    Yorker, 51 (15 September), 122-30.
         Humboldt's Gift seems to promise "a wonderfully animated
    meditation upon the sociological question of the intellec-
    tual's place in America," but it becomes diverted to ques-
    tions of death and immortality. It provides compelling
    characters, like Cantabile, who in the end become bores.
    It begins with issues, but ends in effusion. Bellow's
    style, even, "feels fallen away from a former angelic
    height." The novel is rich in information and speculation;
    but, while there are many surprises, there are no
    revelations.

42 WISSE, RUTH R. "The Schlemiel as Liberal Humanist," in The
    Schlemiel as Modern Hero. Chicago: University of Chicago
    Press, pp. 92-107.
         Bellow portrays many schlemiels in his fiction--indi-
    viduals honestly, but comically, struggling to define them-
    selves as individuals in a world where the possibilities of
    doing so are diminished. His most typical and most clearly
    developed schlemiel is Herzog. Herzog follows the pattern
    of loser-as-victor, of the one who never fails in his final
    self-acceptance. Herzog is set apart by his intelligence
    and self-consciousness; he elucidates and clarifies his own
    feelings. He is finally "the character who lives according
    to a twofold perception of himself in relation to the world,
    both giant and dwarf, alien and center of the universe,
    failure and success, cuckold and great lover, intellectual
    and schlemiel."
         Reprinted in Rovit, ed.: 1975.A4.

1976 A BOOKS

1 GOLDEN, SUSAN LANDAU. "The Novels of Saul Bellow: A Study in
   Development." Ph.D. dissertation, Duke University, 200 pp.
   Listed in Dissertation Abstracts International, 36
   (7: January), 4489A (Order No. 75-29501).
        Focuses on the philosophic development of Saul Bellow,
   tracing his movement from an existentialism in the early

novels to a detailed humanistic alternative to existentialism in the later novels.

1976 B SHORTER WRITINGS

1   ANON. "A Laureate for Bellow." Time, 108 (1 November), 91.
       A profile of Bellow with biographical details upon his
    being awarded the Novel Prize for Literature. His "chief
    heresy has been committed against the century old tradition
    of despair in Western literature." As a novelist Bellow
    has pleased his readers "precisely by not giving the public
    what it thinks it wants."

2   BAKER, C. "Bellow's Gift." Theology Today, 32 (January),
    411-13.
       Bellow used his friend Delmore Schwartz as a model for
    Humboldt in Humboldt's Gift. They became friends during
    their year together in the Creative Arts Program at Prince-
    ton. And Charles Citrine is "more or less a self-portrait
    of Bellow from youth to sexagenarian." Bellow spares
    neither Humboldt nor Citrine. Citrine defends himself and
    his predicament through his metaphysical speculations. The
    book is both serious and funny; its tone is "bright, brash,
    humorous, profane, contemporaneous...."

3   CASEY, J. B. "Bellow's Gift." Virginia Quarterly Review,
    5 (Winter, 1976), 150-54.
       The issue in Humboldt's Gift is "whether or not people
    have the imagination to conceive of life as more than the
    bodies it is written on." For Bellow the mind is the sole
    source of meaning; "There is only the life of the imagina-
    tive mind, playing over the apparent world, taking into
    itself the color and tone of emotion, speculating, analyz-
    ing, sifting its own disparate and colorful materials."

4   CLEMONS, WALTER. "Bellow the Word King." Newsweek, 88
    (1 November), 89.
       A profile of Bellow, with biographical details, upon his
    being awarded the Novel Prize for Literature. Bellow is
    considered one of the most intelligent of American novel-
    ists, and also one of the most sensual. He may be "the
    best exponent since Charles Dickens of monomaniac
    eccentricity."

5   GITENSTEIN, ROSE. "Versions of the Yiddish Literary Tradition
    in Jewish American Literature: Issac Bashevis Singer,
    Abraham Cahan, and Saul Bellow." Ph.D. dissertation, Uni-
    versity of North Carolina, 322 pp. Listed in Dissertation

Abstracts International, 36 (10: April), 6683A
(Order No. 76-9249).
Much closer to Yiddishism than Singer, Bellow adapts
character types and literary forms from the Yiddish literary tradition of the nineteenth century.

6   GOLD, HERBERT. "Bellow's Gift: A Powerful Portrait of
    Israel." Los Angeles Times Book Review (17 October),
    pp. 1, 7.
         In To Jerusalem and Back: A Personal Account Bellow's
    theme "of generosity and concern for others is dramatized
    with stunning simplicity and power." In some ways, the
    book is like a novel, filled with Bellow-type characters
    who are both charming and filled with suffering. In its
    passion and concern, the book reveals what life in Israel
    means today.

7   HOWARD, MAUREEN. Review of Humboldt's Gift. Yale Review, 65
    (Spring), 411-12.
         Humboldt's Gift is a novel about success, an uninterest-
    ing work where talk is cheap. The wit and tension that
    could have been in the novel disappeared with Humboldt's
    death.

8   HOWE, IRVING. Review of To Jerusalem and Back. New York
    Times Book Review (17 October), pp. 1-2.
         Bellow's personal account of Israel is both impassioned
    and thoughtful; it is an important study of one of the most
    tragic and complex issues of our time. It shows Bellow's
    keenness as a listener, and his delight in the liveliness
    of the Israelis. Although he "succumbs a few times to
    moods of apocalypse," his voice is mellower than in the
    past, and his sketches evoking places, ideas, and people
    are wonderful.

9   KANFER, STEFAN. "Tour de Force." Time, 108 (8 November),
    106-07.
         To Jerusalem and Back is typical Bellow: "Part medita-
    tion, part crank letter, tinged with the doubt of Ecclesi-
    astes and the faith of Moses, full of quicksilver insights
    and deep Talmudic scholarship." Bellow raises the ques-
    tions of Israel with talent, grace, and conscience: he is
    particularly successful "in his evocation of an emotional
    landscape."

10 KAZIN, ALFRED. "From Sweden to America: Mr. Bellow's Planet."
    The New Republic, 175 (6 November), 6-8.

1976

> Some might be surprised at Bellow's winning the Nobel
> Prize since he is so "familiar" a novelist. Although the
> central interest in Bellow's development as a novelist has
> been to create protagonists who are intellectuals, he has
> created characters and situations which are vivid and pain-
> fully true. "We recognize them and we are there. So much
> ordinariness no doubt invites condescension and even sur-
> prise." But his gift is that he has led us to see the
> world with his eyes.

11 LEONARD, JOHN. "Novelist Deals with Jews in America." New
    York Times (22 October), pp. 1, A10.
        An appraisal of Bellow's life and work upon his being
    awarded the Nobel Prize for Literature. "If Saul Bellow
    didn't exist, someone exactly like him would have had to
    have been invented, just after the Second World War, by
    New York intellectuals, in a backroom at Partisan Review."
    Although he does not know what to do with his tragic sense
    of life, Bellow is a remarkable novelist, one who has
    "authenticated the experience of American intellectuals in
    the 20th Century."

12 McSWEENEY, KERRY. "Saul Bellow and the Life to Come."
    Critical Quarterly, 18 (Spring), 67-72.
        With its theme of Citrine's spiritual growth, Humboldt's
    Gift differs from Bellow's earlier novels "in its advocacy
    of transcendental postulates." In his quest, Citrine has
    both reality instructors (Renata, Cantabile) and an in-
    structor in the ideal (Humboldt). Bellow is not altogether
    successful in developing this theme: the novel suffers from
    digressive exuberance of narrative incident, from a lack of
    distance between Citrine and the reader, and in Bellow's
    difficulty in dramatizing the process of Citrine's spiritual
    growth.

13 PRESCOTT, PETER S. "Passage to Zion." Newsweek, 88
    (25 October), 108, 110.
        To Jerusalem and Back is a knowledgeable, yet stern and
    demanding book: "the most precise reading I know of the
    psychological climate in Israel today." In the book Bellow
    takes the role of an observer, discursive in his writing,
    waiting to see what will develop.

14 TODD, RICHARD. Review of Humboldt's Gift. Atlantic, 237
    (January), 96.
        Humboldt's Gift is a grand novel, suffering perhaps
    "from perplexing contrivances of plot," but sustained by
    its high spirited intelligence.

Index

INDEX

"Ha-Professor Eino Me'uban: Cohav Ha-Lekhet Shel Mar Sammler Me'et Saul Bellow," 1971.B9

Hardwick, Elizabeth, 1948.B4; 1959.B13

Harper, Gordon Lloyd, 1966.B24; 1967.B14

Harper, Howard Morrall, Jr., 1965.B29; 1967.B15; 1971.B11

Harris, James N., 1972.B9

Hartman, Hugh C., 1968.A3

Harwell, Meade, 1954.B6

Hasenclever, Walter, 1961.B6

Hassan, Ihab H., 1960.B4; 1961.B7; 1966.B25-26

Hays, Peter L., 1971.B12

Hebrew criticism, 1971.B9

Heiney, Donald, 1972.B10

"Heirs of the Tradition," 1964.B1

Hemingway and Bellow compared, 1969.B16; 1972.B3

"Henderson's Bellow," 1959.B35

Henderson the Rain King,
  Considered with other novels, 1960.B2, B4-5; 1963.B1, B4, B18; 1964.B34, B44, B60; 1965.A1, B23; 1966.B21; 1967.A7, B1, B15, B22, B27-28; 1968.A1; 1970.B53; 1971.A1, B7-8, B21, B35; 1972.A3; 1973.B35; 1974.A1, A3; 1975.B26, B38
  Reviews, 1959.B1, B3-16, B18-19, B22-23, B25-31, B33, B35-42; 1960.B8-9, B11; 1961.B2, B5-6, B8-9, B12; 1962.B11; 1964.B15, 1966.B45
  Single studies, 1960.B6; 1961.B1; 1962.B2; 1965.B28; 1966.B15, B25; 1969.B7, B17; 1970.B9, B47; 1971.B14, B22-23, B27, B33; 1972.B5, B20, B23; 1973.B10, B24, B31; 1974.B2; 1975.B5

"Henderson the Rain King: A Major Theme and a Technical Problem," 1970.B9

"Henderson the Rain King and William James," 1971.B14

"Henderson the Rain King: An Orchestration of Soul Music," 1972.B20

"Henderson the Rain King, Eliot, and Browning," 1971.B33

Hendricks, George, 1970.B25

Heppenstall, Rayner, 1946.B1

"The Hero as Jew: Reflections on Herzog," 1968.B3

Heroic Fiction: The Epic Tradition and the Novels of the Twentieth Century, 1971.B21

The Heroic Ideal in American Literature, 1971.B7

"A Hero Sick with Abstractions," 1964.B16

Herzog,
  Considered with other novels, 1965.A1, B21-22; 1966.B11, B34, B47; 1967.A7, B2, B4, B15, B22, B27-28; 1968.A1, B16, B25; 1969.A2-3, B6, B15; 1970.B53; 1971.A1, B7-8, B21, B25, B35; 1972.A3; 1973.B4, B35; 1974.A1, A3; 1975.B26, B38
  Reviews, 1964.B5-B7, B11-13, B16, B19, B21, B23, B25, B27-30, B35-37, B41-42, B45-46, B48, B50-54, B59, B61-68, B70-71, B73, B75; 1965.B2-3, B6-7, B12, B14, B24-25, B30, B32-35, B37, B42-44, B47, B50-52, B54-56, B58-60, B63; 1966.B17-18, B20, B31-32; 1967.B20-21, B24-25; 1969.B11
  Single studies, 1965.B11, B53, B62; 1966.B2, B46; 1968.B3, B24; 1969.B4, B14, B18, B20, B22; 1970.B17; 1971.B13, B15, B24, B30; 1972.B16; 1973.B34

"Herzog," 1964.B66

"Herzog and the Passion," 1965.B14

"Herzog: A Transcendental Solution to an Existential Problem," 1969.B22

Herzog in Front of a Mirror," 1964.B23

"Interpretation of Jewish Char-
acter in Renaissance and
Recent Literature," 1974.B12
Interviews with Bellow, 1963.B3,
B8; 1964.B14, B38-39, B49,
B55, B72; 1965.B20; 1966.B24,
B29; 1967.B9, B14; 1971.B6;
1972.B14, B21; 1973.B21
"An Interview with Saul Bellow,"
1963.B8
"Introducing an Important New
Writer," 1944.B8
"Introspective Stinker," 1944.B1
Invention of the Jew: Jewish
American Education Novels,
1969.B27
Isaac, Dan, 1965.B30
Italian criticism, 1956.B17;
1957.B14; 1959.B6; 1965.B36;
1966.B7
"The It and the We," 1975.B7
Iwamoto, Iwao, 1972.B12
Iwayama, Tajiro, 1972.B13

Jacobson, Dan, 1959.B16
Japanese criticism, 1970.B44;
1972.B11-13, B24
Jefchak, Andrew, 1974.B8
Jensen, Emily, 1963.B12
"The Jew as American," 1966.B9
"The Jewish Author Looks at the
Black," 1973.B16
"The Jewish Heritage in Contempo-
rary American Fiction,"
1963.B9
Jewishness and Jewish themes in
Bellow's novels, 1948.B2;
1957.B9; 1958.B4; 1959.B2,
B32, B34; 1961.B4; 1962.B12;
1963.B9; 1964.B20, B53;
1965.B9, B14, B38, B51;
1966.B5, B36, B41; 1967.B10-
11, B17; 1968.B3, B23-24;
1969.B16, B27; 1970.B30;
1972.B7; 1975.B5, B42
"Jewishness, Judaism, and the
American Jewish Novelist,"
1965.B9
"The Jewishness of Bellow's
Henderson," 1975.B5

The Jewish Writer in America:
Assimilation and the Crisis
of Identity, 1971.B8
"Jewish Writers in America: A
Place in the Establishment,"
1961.B4
Jews and Americans, 1965.B38
"The Jew's Complaint in Recent
American Fiction: Beyond
Exodus and Still in the
Wilderness," 1972.B7
Jones, D. A. N., 1966.B28
Jones, David R., 1970.B36
Josipovici, Gabriel, 1971.B15
Jotterand, Franck, 1966.B29
"A Journey to the Interior,"
1962.B2
Joyce and Bellow compared,
1965.B50; 1966.B20, B42;
1968.B3; 1973.B19
"Judea-kei Sakka no Miryoku--
Bellow to Malamud," 1972.B12

Kalb, Bernard, 1953.B16
Kanfer, Stefan, 1976.B9
Kar, Parfulla C., 1973.A1
Katz, Bill, 1968.B7
Kazin, Alfred, 1956.B13; 1959.B17-
18; 1962.B3; 1963.B13;
1965.B31; 1966.B30; 1968.B8;
1970.B37; 1971.B16; 1973.B14;
1976.B10
Kermode, Frank, 1965.B32
Kiely, Robert, 1970.B38
"King Saul," 1964.B64
Kirsch, Robert, 1975.B17
Klausler, Alfred, 1975.B18
Klein, Marcus, 1962.B4-5;
1963.B14; 1964.B48; 1975.A4
Knipp, Thomas R., 1969.B17
Knoke, Paul D., 1971.B17
Kogan, Herman, 1959.B19; 1964.B49
"Koheleth in Chicago: The Quest
for the Real in 'Looking for
Mr. Green,'" 1974.B11
"Košmarna Farsa O Žrtvi Sola
Beloua," 1973.B11
Kramer, Maurice, 1967.B17
Kristol, Irving, 1944.B5;
1954.B8
Kroll, Jack, 1975.B9

INDEX

INDEX

INDEX

Index

"White Man's Black Man: Three Views," 1973.B27

Whitman and Bellow compared, 1967.B30

Whittemore, Reed, 1959.B41

"Who Killed Herzog? or Three American Novelists," 1966.B36

Wieting, Molly S., 1970.A5

Williams, Patricia W., 1973.A3

Wilson, Angus, 1954.B14; 1959.B42

Wilson, Edmund, 1944.B12; 1971.B20

Winegarten, R., 1965.B61; 1966.B48

Wisse, Ruth R., 1970.B62; 1975.B42

"The Woes of Herzog," 1965.B47

"The Women in Augie March," 1968.B13

Women in Bellow's fiction, 1960.B1; 1968.B13; 1971.B30; 1974.B3; 1975.B38

"The World of Saul Bellow," 1959.B18

"Writer and the Common World," 1965.B46

"Writers of Half-Talent," 1957.B5

"Writing American Fiction," 1961.B11

Wyndham, Francis, 1957.B18

Young, James Dean, 1965.B62

"Zetsubo no Kanata ni," 1970.B44

Zietlow, E. R., 1973.B35

Zinnes, Harriet, 1965.B63